STAR·WARS™

RETURN OF THE
JEDI
™

THE ORIGINAL RADIO DRAMA

Other Star Wars books available:

THE ART OF STAR WARS - A NEW HOPE EPISODE IV
THE ART OF STAR WARS - THE EMPIRE STRIKES BACK EPISODE V
THE ART OF STAR WARS - THE RETURN OF THE JEDI EPISODE VI
THE ART OF STAR WARS GALAXY
THE ART OF STAR WARS GALAXY 2
STAR WARS - THE ORIGINAL RADIO DRAMA
STAR WARS - THE EMPIRE STRIKES BACK -
THE ORIGINAL RADIO DRAMA

STAR WARS™
RETURN OF THE JEDI™

THE ORIGINAL RADIO DRAMA

**Based on Characters and Situations
Created by George Lucas
And on the screenplay by Lawrence Kasdan
and George Lucas**

Radio Play by Brian Daley

With an Introduction by Anthony Daniels

TITAN BOOKS

STAR WARS: RETURN OF THE JEDI
THE ORIGINAL RADIO DRAMA

ISBN 1 85286 737 X

Published by
Titan Books Ltd
42-44 Dolben Street
London SE1 0UP

First Titan edition November 1996
2 4 6 8 10 9 7 5 3 1

Star Wars ® TM & © 1996 Lucasfilm Ltd. All Rights Reserved.
Published originally in the United States by Ballantine Books Inc.

British Library Cataloguing-in-Publication Data.
A catalogue record for this book is available from the British Library.

Printed and bound in Great Britain by Cox and Wyman Ltd, Reading, Berkshire.

INTRODUCTION

It was more than ten years after we had finished the radio version of *The Empire Strikes Back* when the phone rang. I hadn't actually been sitting by it, waiting, but it was good to hear Mel Sahr's voice again.

Mel had been one of the main motivating forces behind the original *Star Wars* and *The Empire Strikes Back* radio series for National Public Radio. I remember the fun we had making them and the continuing unease I felt that we had never completed this incarnation of the trilogy, otherwise so fully represented in every merchandise-filled bedroom of every *Star Wars* fan across the world.

In those pre–*Star Wars* days, my childhood had been partly spent staring, not at a movie or TV screen, but at the Bakelite grille of a wireless set. *Journey into Space* had been a particularly chilling and graphic experience broadcast by the BBC. Each week our family sat around the glowing dial, picturing the horrors and dangers of man's first landing on the planet Mars and his meeting with the first alien life-forms ever encountered. No movie monster has ever been so terrifying.

Years later, my first acting contract was with the BBC in London, as a member of the Radio Drama Repertory Company. They produce hundreds of drama productions a year. I loved it there. There is something completely magical about creating pictures only with sound. It doesn't matter if you look like a weed, you can still play a bronze-biceped hero on the radio. I did.

Given my long association with radio I was glad to be a part of NPR's *Star Wars* serial. For a start, I didn't have to wear the gold suit. But more than that, I felt it presented the wonderful story that George Lucas had created in a form available to anyone who had access to a radio. No admission charges, no standing in line, no stench of popcorn. Just the actors' voices, Tom Voegeli's effects and your imagination. It worked splendidly. So, too, did *Empire*.

Then silence. For ten years.

Mel explained that NPR's financing problems had held back the completion of the project with the intended production of *Return of the Jedi*. Now Sallie Neall, producer for HighBridge Audio, had managed to create a budget that made it possible once more. A major hurdle had been flattened. Hitherto unpublished passages of John Williams's outstanding music score would be available. Three hours of radio employ staves more music than a two-hour movie, unless you want to hear the same notes over and over again. Mel told me that a production was now viable. *Would I care to be involved?* Was Brian Daley writing the scripts? *Yes, he was.* Yes, I would.

Months later I was sitting in a boardroom in Los Angeles with Lucasfilm's Director of Publishing, Lucy Autrey Wilson, Mel, Tom, and John Madden, who had so happily directed our previous efforts. A problem had arisen. Brian was sick and couldn't join us. He had been fighting cancer for some time. He was very sorry not to be with us at the script conference.

There are always rewrites in any project. Particularly, in this case, there were all sorts of tangential continuity restrictions effected by the future prequels and projects in Lucasfilm's plans. So John Whitman had come along, not only with his writing skills but with his depth of knowledge about the trilogy. We each had lists of comments and suggestions. Many vanished as John Madden and I hammed up the lines between us and made Brian's writing come alive, just the way he'd written them. Perhaps, because we both had jet lag, we were hammier than usual, but the room constantly sounded with raucous laughter at Brian's humorous inventions. I won't preempt them here, but do look out for Leia's throw-away about her skimpy costume—and, too, watch out for the inflammatory "luggage" insult.

Studying the scripts, it was clear just how difficult it is to describe filmic scenes only in sound. Imagine trying this with Jabba's palace—a nightmare in all senses of the word. Brian had given me a problem. He had cleverly decided to put a lot of the description into a conversation between Threepio and another character, lurking in that mass of strange creatures. Unfortunately he had made my companion Boba Fett. I argued that I had always had a slight problem with the "cheat" of having Boba speak at all. I could accept that it was a necessity, but for him to bond so closely with Threepio was pushing unreality a bit too far. So, in a nifty pinch from Timothy Zahn's *Tales from Jabba's Palace*, we changed Boba for Arica, an exotic beauty whom we assumed to be partying-on in the unseemly melee. Jabba's film subtitles were not a problem as Threepio naturally made them his own. But sometimes, when the great Jabba is particularly disgusting, his own Huttese speaks louder than any translation.

And, of course, there were my lines. I'd always loved the way Brian had developed Threepio's character in the radio scripts. Everyone's lines have to be expanded from the movies, since they need to paint in the visuals. But Brian had a real ability to capture Threepio's strange mixture of humourless comedy, his oddly bleak but loving personality. No other writer has been able to do this for Threepio, outside his movie incarnation. Only Brian, at the end of

Left to right: Perry, Julie, Ann, Tom, John, Mel (front), Anthony, and Josh.

the Ewok storytelling scene, could find a radio way of capturing the droid's deeply felt frustration with Han Solo.

So there we were again, Ann Sachs (Leia), and Perry King (Han), and everyone was lying that no one looked ten years older than the last time we'd met. Mind you, the moody lighting at Westlake Audio Studios hid most of the wrinkles. It was still geared more toward heavy-metal musicians than golden metal droids and their need to see the script.

A happy new addition to the team was Josh Fardon, who had joined us to play Luke Skywalker, so at least one member of the cast was the right age for the part. With Arye Gross playing Lando, I was the only original member of the movie cast present in the studio. Would I be able to restrain myself from giving helpful advice? The question never arose. All the members of the team made the scripts and characters their own, without any assistance from me. Anyway, John Madden gracefully masterminded the scenes so all of us felt comfortably supported by the genial atmosphere created by his confident direction.

Tom needed to keep everyone's tracks separated for eventual post-production in his Minnesota studios. As usual, I spent the days isolated behind glass screens, listening to the drama unfold around me through headphones. I wasn't the only one. Brock Peters as Vader and the even more fearsome Emperor, Paul Hecht, were similarly banished to various undignified corners and cupboards as Tom ran out of studio space. When you hear the echoingly bleak acoustics of the Emperor's throne room, imagine Paul in a tiny store-cupboard draped in blankets. Tom provides the rest. What did have us all craning our necks for a better view down a corridor was Edward Asner giving his most outrageously disgusting rendition of Jabba the Hutt. Remarkably, no mechanical aids were used in his performance. It paints a perfect picture in any listener's ear of one of *Jedi*'s most hilarious characters.

It says a lot about the acting that off-duty members of the cast would cram into the small control room to listen to what was going on in the studio. Tom's infinite patience helped him to concentrate. He just kept going, carefully monitoring each take of the performances being recorded on the multichannels of digital tape, in spite of the raucously distracting appreciation of the growing crowds. In particular, John Lithgow's delightful re-creation of Yoda was standing-room-only.

Of course there is always the strange contrast between what observers see through the studio window and what it sounds like over the speakers. We all looked very silly as we contorted our bodies, trying to suggest we had been caught in an Ewok net trap. It sounds convincing though. So does Han's passionate ardour. Perry is an old hand at radio passion—I remember it was not always so. But now at a mere hint of stage direction he can, apparently, sweep a sighing Princess Leia into his arms and cover her lips with lavish kisses. The truth is more prosaic: Perry at mike three, Ann at mike four, some feet away. Perry holding his script in his left hand while leaning closer to the mike. Ann holding her script and breathing heavily. Perry's right hand comes up to his lips. His breathing gets really heavy. He kisses the back of

Left to right: Arye, Ann, and Perry.

Scott Windus Photography

his hand, passionately. Ann sighs and goes *mmmmm*. In the control room it sounds like total *amour*. In the studio everyone rolls around in helpless mirth.

As in the movies, much work was left to post-production. Anyone having a conversation with Artoo-Detoo was on his own. Artoo's beeps would be added later. The Ewoks would similarly arrive on tape from Ben Burtt, their original audio creator. Actually, some things are better heard and not seen. Personally, I think Ewoks look great on radio. It had been intended that the crowd tracks should also be lifted from established recordings. Fortunately John Madden decided to employ a group of actors to cackle and snarl as we went along. The studio simply came alive. They were hilarious to hear but even better to watch as they re-created the scum of Jabba's entourage. Later, they became the macho crowd of pilots in the briefing room with Mon Mothma. Talk about versatility. Even Howard Roffman, Lucasfilm's Vice President of Licensing, was persuaded to join in as part of the Rebel Alliance. He couldn't quite understand that everyone speaks at the same time in a radio crowd. He kept listening to the others very politely, and nodding. Nodding does not work on radio. Howard is not natural radio material.

It must be so easy on the radio. You don't have to learn the lines. How many times have I heard that. The truth is different. For a start, most films have only some blue-screen effects. Radio is all blue-screen. The actors have to imagine everything. Pretending you are on the lushly verdant Moon of Endor when you are, in fact, in a tiny mirrored booth on Beverley Boulevard takes some doing. As for learning lines, if you aren't absolutely familiar with them and their position on the script page, you'd never be able to take your eyes off it. Most actors are very insecure people; they need to look at each other. If you don't know the script, you're bound to lose your place, with a resulting, embarrassing pause. My problem is that I never learned to write neatly. All my notes and changes and self-instructions are like hieroglyphs and render the neatly typed pages into penciled labyrinths. One aspect that I noticed in these scripts was the size of the characters' words relative to the size of the stage directions. Though Tom would deny it, it must tell us something about who is more important on the radio. Somebody in production had made a judgment, even before we started.

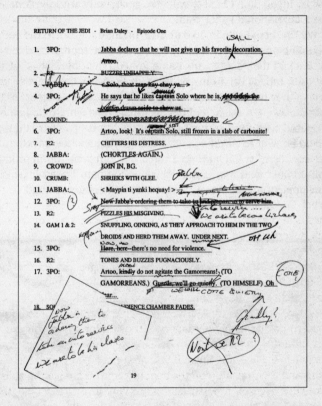

. . . my notes and changes and self-instructions are like hieroglyphs and render the neatly typed pages into penciled labyrinths . . .

So recording went on for the six days, surviving various attacks. The studio sounded like a hospital as most of the cast coughed and sneezed their way through boxes of tissues and throat sweets. A greater attack came from various photo and TV crews, doing their jobs but certainly distracting us from ours. NPR led the assault, as we all recorded money-begging promos on its behalf. If you didn't hear them, give generously anyway. America needs its National Public Radio.

We had kept Brian up to date with phone calls, but at the end of recording on the last Saturday, various cast members scribbled on the back of their scripts and came up with their own lines, which we then taped. Far from trying to show Brian that anyone can write if they have a pencil, rather, our jottings were a tribute to his imagination, his skills, and his personality, which we had all appreciated with fond admiration over the years. The finished tape would be sent to Brian as our way of saying *You were with us all the way*. Tom would later do a rapid but excellent 70mm production number with music and effects on the bare material, which I now present to you. I'm sure my fellow writers won't mind.

Anthony Daniels

(MUSIC: STAR WARS THEME CRASHES IN. HOLD & FADE UNDER)

LIVELY CROWD: From the Rebel Alliance, Brian. We wish you were here. *(LOUD CHEERS AND CATCALLS) (CHANTING)* Bri-an. Bri-an. Bri-an. Bri-an. Bri-an. Bri-an. Bri-an. *(FADING UNDER AS MUSIC FADES UP & HOLDS)*

(MUSIC FADES UNDER)

LEIA: *(URGENTLY)* This is Princess Leia Organa transmitting to Brian Daley on Earth. We seem to be having a bit of a time warp here. Luke seems to be shedding years as he matures into a Jedi Knight and . . .

HAN: *(INTERRUPTING)* Leia?

LEIA: Han?

HAN: Are you talking to Brian?

LEIA: Uhhuh.

HAN: You . . . You love him, don't you?

LEIA: *(LONG PAUSE)* Well, *yes*.

HAN: *(PAUSE)* Fine. I understand. When he comes back, I won't get in your way.

LEIA: Han. He's the *writer*.

HAN: The writer! Then you weren't . . . well . . . But then, Brian isn't . . . ?

LEIA: *(INTERRUPTING)* Why don't you just stop worrying about Brian and . . . kiss me.

HAN: Uh Leia. Uhhh. *(HE KISSES THE BACK OF HIS HAND WITH ARDOUR)*

LEIA: Uhh mhhh. Urgh! Aggh! *(GRUNTING & SWEATING FX)(JABBA MUSIC FADES UP UNDER)* Get that tongue off me! You vile—*thing*, you! *(SHE LAUGHS, UNABLE TO CONTAIN HER MIRTH ANY LONGER. A REAL PRO)*

PERRY: *(LAUGHING)* Hey Brian!

PERRY & ANNE: We love you. And we miss you.

JOHN MADDEN: *(ECHOING, AS IF FROM A GALAXY FAR, FAR AWAY)* We miss youuuu . . .

(MUSIC GETS MORE SINISTER)(FADE UP PALACE CROWD ATMOS) (DISGUSTING NOISES)

JABBA: Yabriannndaley gommmakikochh. Ggehhht welllllll. *(HE FALLS ASLEEP, SNORING)*

SALACIOUS CRUMB: *(CACKLES WITH HYSTERICAL MIRTH)*

(PALACE FADES UNDER AS MUSIC CROSS FADES TO BATTLE THEME)

R2: *(EMERGENCY WHOOPS)*

LUKE: Artoo. Prepare to lay a course on the navicomputer.

R2: ??*!!?

LUKE: What? My part?

R2: !

LUKE: No, it's fine. I just took over for another actor.

R2: *??

LUKE: No, it doesn't hurt. I won't let it. Okay. Course plotted. Get ready to jump into hyperspace.

R2: **?

LUKE: That's right. We're going to go to the Baltimore system. I have a promise to keep—to an old friend. Look, actually, I've never met the guy. But do you think I'm going to pass up an opportunity like this . . . *(PROXIMITY ALERT STARTS SPEEDING UP)*

JOHN MADDEN: *(INTERRUPTING)* Okay. Okay. *(CUT FX)* I just want to do one pickup, Tom. Can we just go please from . . . "Your mother's a set of matched luggage." Stand by. *(LAUGHS)* Hi, Brian . . . *(LAUGHS. HE CAN'T GO ON. ANOTHER REAL PRO)* OK. Cut. Thanks.

TOM: *(OVER TALKBACK) (LAUGHING)* Great!

(VADER THEME SMASHES IN. VADER BREATHES UP CLOSE)

VADER: Greetings, Brian. I kneel before you and await your orders to execute your wish. *(FADE BREATHING & MUSIC UNDER)*

BROCK: *(CONTINUING)* Brian, this is Brock . . . Get well . . . Rejoin us, soon . . . Love . . .

(FADE UP EMPEROR'S THEME & HOLD UNDER)

EMPEROR: *(CHILLING ACOUSTIC)* Brian . . . Your overlord the Emperor is pleased . . . with his lines, and commands you to get well, be well, to stay well . . .

(FADE MUSIC)

(ECHOING ATMOS)

R2: *** ** *

(SERVO MOTORS APPROACHING)

3PO: *(CALLING)* Artoo? Artoo-Detoo! What are you doing here, in an empty studio?

R2: ** ** * *** *

3PO: Rehearsing for your next scene? But Artoo, we have finished recording *Return of the Jedi.*

R2: ***

3PO: Oh don't be sad, Artoo. We had a lot of fun, didn't we. And all because of Master Brian.

R2: *** ***

3PO: Yes. I think he did an *excellent* job. But . . . well . . . I think he gave you rather too many lines.

R2: !

3PO: Just you watch your language!

R2: ** *** **!

3PO: Ohh. That is a good idea, Artoo. Um, let me see. Um, um. *(TAPS THE MICROPHONE TENTATIVELY)* Hello? Um.

R2: **

3PO: Um. Ready? *(CONFIDENTLY)* Master Brian. Artoo and I want to say that it has been a distinct honor and a *joy* to work with you.

R2: *

3PO: With our thanks, we send you our very *best* wishes. *(PAUSES. THEN TO ARTOO)* There!

R2: ***??

3PO: No you can't have another retake, Artoo! Oh really! *(HIS VOICE FADES AS THEY LEAVE)* The trouble with you is, Hollywood has affected your circuits. You have become ridiculously starstru . . . *(A DISTANT DOOR CLOSES BEHIND THEM)*

(SILENCE)

We met for dinner that night in a lively restaurant on Melrose. Strangely for an LA eatery, we could hear each other speak— maybe we'd all got used to shouting over intergalactic battles and explosions. As soon as the wine hit the glasses we raised them in a toast to absent friends—to Brian. HighBridge, in the guise of Julie Hartley, our coproducer, were the kind hosts, so quite a few glasses were subsequently downed in the happy relief that a wrap party usually brings. But there is always a tinge of sadness on these occasions. You never know if you'll meet again. A bit like the end of *E.T.* with no guaranteed sequel. I had admired every member of the cast and crew for their skill, persistence, and good humour and for their part in the general bonhomie of the production. It had been fun. But, for the cast at least, it was over.

We left for our various homes and hotels. Ann and I hitched a ride in Perry's extravagantly mud-encrusted AT-AT land cruiser, which, I'm glad to say, he maneuvered with the sort of care and skill he'd shown flying the *Falcon*. So we arrived back safely. We said farewell. Maybe someone said May the Force be with you. I don't know. I went to bed.

My phone woke me the next morning. It was John Madden. He'd just heard that Brian had died that night as we sat in the restaurant—just about the time we were drinking to absent friends—to Brian.

When Tom's finished tape reached me in London a week later he had enclosed a note.

To the cast and crew of Return of the Jedi for radio

It was with the greatest sadness that we heard about Brian Daley's death—within hours of the very successful end of our recording his scripts.

It seemed the only appropriate thing to do was to go ahead and put together your message to him. Although this tape was meant to be heard by Brian in our world, we can only hope that he knows the love expressed on it in another.

Love Tom

It had become a joke that Threepio usually stole the last line of any scene that included him in Brian's scripts. In doing so here, I cannot better Tom's sentiments—without Brian to write the lines for me.

London, March 1996

Brian Daley

EPISODE ONE:
"TATOOINE HAUNTS"

CAST:
Threepio
Luke
Darth Vader
Emperor Palpatine
Bib Fortuna
Jabba The Hutt
Ninedenine
Arica
Oola
Boushh (Leia)
Han

SOUND/FX ROLES:
Artoo-Detoo
Gamorrean #1
Gamorrean #2
Max Rebo's Band
Salacious Crumb
Power Droid
Rancor
Chewbacca

ANNOUNCER: OPENING CREDITS.

Music: Opening theme.

NARRATOR: A long time ago in a galaxy far, far away there came a time of revolution, when Rebels united to challenge a tyrannical Empire. Since its defeats at Hoth and elsewhere, the Rebel Alliance has rallied to press the Empire hard. Interstellar war hangs in the balance, and all combatants feel that final, decisive battle draws near. Preparing himself for this moment, Luke Skywalker has trained tenaciously and undergone many trials in his efforts to become a Jedi Knight and learn the ways of the Force.

Sound: The sand-winds of Tatooine in the background.

NARRATOR: Now he has returned to the desert planet Tatooine, where he was raised. It is here that Luke means to stake his life on an attempt to rescue his friend Han Solo from the clutches of the vile, sluglike gangster Jabba the Hutt. But before he is ready to face that challenge, or the greater perils that may lie beyond, he must finish one last task. So it is that the morning light of the planet's twin suns finds him in a hermit's dwelling, hard by the Western Dune Sea.

SCENE 1-1   TATOOINE EXTERIOR

Sound: Luke tinkering with tools. Click of metal on metal, fitting plugs into sockets, small whirr of a handheld drill, turning screw, etc.

Sound: Page turn.

LUKE: Let's see ... *(READING TO HIMSELF)* "The crystal alignment must be precise if the energy beam is to maintain its density . . ."

ARTOO: WHISTLES A QUERY OVER THE END OF THE ABOVE.

LUKE: *(WORKING DISTRACTEDLY)* Hmmm? No, Artoo, I don't need you. I was just reading out loud. Talking to myself, I guess. It's what old Ben used to do, too, sometimes. That's one of the reasons all the kids around Anchorhead thought he was a sun-struck hermit. Must be something about being back on Tatooine, back in his house. *(WORKING ON)* Brings out the crazy old wizard in me, too.

ARTOO: ANIMATED, ALMOST INDIGNANT BEEPS.

LUKE: *(LAUGHING)* If you're saying I can talk to you, Artoo, thanks. But at the moment I need to work on this little project. The sooner I get it done, the better. If Threepio were here, I think he'd call this "mindless tedium."

ARTOO: A DECLARATIVE STREAM OF WHOOPS AND BEEPS.

LUKE: Yeah, well, don't worry, we'll meet up with Threepio and the others soon enough. I had to come back to Ben's house to do this. I needed his tools and books. And it completes the circle somehow.

Sound: Page turn.

LUKE: *(READING TO HIMSELF AGAIN)* "Adegan crystals are recommended for maximum density and purity." Yeah, well, I guess these will do.

Sound: Tinkering stops. Crystals clinking together in his palm, then inserted into metal cylinder. Under next, the cylinder will slip, and all objects will clatter to the ground.

LUKE: *(EFFORT OF CONCENTRATION)* Al . . . most . . . got it— ahhh! Not again! Artoo, get that focal lens for me. It slid under the workbench.

4

ARTOO: A SLIGHTLY IRRITATED STREAM OF CRACKLES AND BOOPS THAT SOUND AN AWFUL LOT LIKE INVECTIVE.

LUKE: I'm sure you're giving me a lot of helpful advice, my little friend, but this is something I have to do on my own. I have to know that I'm ready for this. Ready for what lies ahead.

Sound: Artoo's utility arm extends and there is a 'plink' as the droid drops something on the table.

ARTOO: BLEEPS DUBIOUSLY.

LUKE: Thanks. *(FRUSTRATED)* . . . I don't know, Artoo, maybe this can't be done.

ARTOO: ONE SAD, REMONSTRATIVE WHOOP.

Sound: Tinkering resumes.

LUKE: Give me the book, Artoo. Last try. Either I'm ready for this or I'm not.

Sound: Artoo humming away as Luke tinkers. Page turn.

LUKE: *(READING ALOUD)* "The concave surface of the focal lens must rest within a two-degree arc of . . ." *(STOPS SUDDENLY)* What am I doing? I've read the instructions a dozen times. And a dozen times I have failed. "Always with you it cannot be done." Master Yoda, can I forget so soon? I don't need this.

Sound: Tosses the book aside. He begins to feel the Force guiding him. More tinkering timed to next lines. The tinkering is smooth and steady.

LUKE: Artoo, hand me the superconductor . . .

ARTOO: BLEEPS IN COMPLIANCE.

LUKE: . . . and now the power cell . . .

ARTOO: BLEEPS AGAIN.

LUKE: . . . and the crystals.

Sound: Tinkering accelerates with smooth confidence, there is a final 'click!' of things snapping into place, and all sound stops abruptly.

LUKE: There! It's done.

ARTOO: WHISTLES AND CLICKS A QUERY.

LUKE: "Try not. Do or do not. There is no try." Here goes . . .

Sound: Flick of a switch. Suddenly we hear the unmistakable sound of a lightsaber igniting! It dopplers as Luke whirls it around.

Sound: Lightsaber being extinguished.

LUKE: All right. I'm ready.

SCENE 1-2 INTERIOR EMPEROR'S THRONE ROOM

Sound: Hiss of an automatic door opening. It has a particularly violent quality. This hiss blends into the rasping of Darth Vader's mask as a single pair of heavy, booted feet strike across a metal grill. The feet stop, and clothes rustle as Vader kneels. A pause here filled only by the breath mask. We, and Vader, are waiting.

EMPEROR: He grows strong.

VADER: Yes, my master. I have felt it.

EMPEROR: Perhaps he should have been destroyed on Bespin. It is unlike you to fail in such matters, Lord Vader.

VADER: He will not escape again. He can still be turned. I need only one more opportunity to—

EMPEROR: I have other work for you, my friend. Our efforts near the moon of Endor have fallen behind schedule. Use your particular talents to encourage the engineers to make haste. Impress upon them the importance of meeting my every expectation. You have my permission to make examples.

VADER: I shall leave at once, my master. As for Skywalker—

EMPEROR: He is not your concern. He could be a powerful tool, Lord Vader. My tool. But only if he serves my purpose.

VADER: As you wish, my master.

EMPEROR: Those who do not serve my ends, no matter how powerful they are, will be eliminated. Are we clear on this matter, Lord Vader?

VADER: We are clear.

EMPEROR: Excellent. Leave at once for Endor, and wait for me there.

SCENE 1–3   EXTERIOR TATOOINE

Sound: Sand-winds etc.

THREEPIO: *(MOVING ON)* Artoo, wait for me! Artoo-Detoo, stop! I simply must rest for a moment.

ARTOO: *(MOVING ON, AHEAD OF THREEPIO)* WHIRBLES AND BLEEPS AT THREEPIO TO KEEP MOVING.

THREEPIO: Artoo, you halt this very instant.

Sound: Artoo's drive motors rev down, tread drives make small braking squeals.

ARTOO: CHIRRUPS IRRITABLY.

THREEPIO: That's more like it.

ARTOO: THROWS IN A RASPBERRY.

THREEPIO: You watch your language. Easy for you to say "keep it in gear." You know full well that all this wretched sand is hard on more technologically evolved droids like myself.

Sound: Another moaning gust of sirocco.

THREEPIO: This place will be the end of us yet. How could Master Luke have ordered us out into these murderous wastelands alone? Surely he doesn't expect us to rescue Captain Solo without assistance?

ARTOO: CHITTERS A REMINDER.

THREEPIO: Are you certain your electromagnetic field sensors are functioning correctly?

ARTOO: BURBLES INDIGNANTLY.

THREEPIO: Then where is the palace of Jabba the Hutt? There's nothing here but sand and rock—

ARTOO: *(INTERRUPTING)* WHISTLES FOR THREEPIO'S ATTENTION, CHIRPS A "TALLY-HO."

THREEPIO: Building? What building . . . *(SPYING IT)* Oh! That is scarcely what I would call a palace, Artoo. It looks more like an iron foundry.

ARTOO: FLUTES A QUESTION.

THREEPIO: Of course I'm worried. And you should be, too. Lando Calrissian and poor Chewbacca never returned when they set out for that awful place.

ARTOO: WHISTLES UNCERTAINLY.

THREEPIO: If I told you half the things I've heard about Jabba the Hutt, you'd probably short-circuit. Perhaps there's been some mistake. Let me hear the message Master Luke gave you to convey to Jabba.

ARTOO: REFUSES PRIMLY.

THREEPIO: "Classified?" I am Master Luke's most trusted confidant. He didn't mean you to keep it secret from me.

ARTOO: TWEEDLES A STUBBORN NONCOMPLIANCE.

THREEPIO: I have no intention of arguing until my lubrication fittings clog up. Come along, let's get this over with.

Sound: Tatooine fades for transition.

SCENE 1–4   EXTERIOR JABBA'S PALACE GATE

Sound: Groaning and squeaking of rusty armorplate walls pressured by the sandsquall winds. Distant, ominous grinding. Boiler room pounding.

THREEPIO: What a forbidding place! Artoo, are you sure this is the right spot?

ARTOO: REAFFIRMS IT CURTLY.

THREEPIO: Oh. Well, I don't see a comlink terminal. I suppose I'd better knock.

Sound: Threepio's metal knuckles echoing on the metal hull of the palace.

THREEPIO: *(WITHOUT WAITING)* Ah, nobody home.

Sound: A small circular fitting on the great iron portal unlatches, slides aside, under next.

THREEPIO: We'd better depart right away and inform Master Luke . . . eh? *(REACTS OVER NEXT)*

Sound: Clacking and ratcheting, angry snapping open of a protective metal "eyelid," as a mechanical arm telescopes out of the aperture, then snaps open to expose its eyeball cam.

THREEPIO: Goodness gracious me! A monitor arm!

EYEBALL: *(VIA INTERCOM)* <Tee chee tad un gootah!>

Sound: The door-periscope swings and angles, inspecting the droids from all angles and distances, under next.

THREEPIO: Mind it doesn't poke out your photoreceptor, Artoo! *(REACTS TO CAM ARM)* And you watch where you're swiveling, you hyperactive macroscanner!

Sound: A pop of static as the cam's intercom activates.

EYEBALL: *(VIA INTERCOM)* <By choo ahd bin kee!>

THREEPIO: It speaks Twi'lek. *(TO THE CAM)* Er, <Artoo Detoowha bo Seethreepiowha ey toota odd mishka Jabba du Hutt.>

EYEBALL: *(VIA INTERCOM)* <Kuju gwankee? Mypee gaza. O-ho, ho, ho ho!>

Sound: Intercom crackles, switching off, static ceasing. Cam eye snaps shut, mechanical arm retracts back into door fitting.

THREEPIO: *(REACTS)*

ARTOO: TWEEDLES INDIGNANTLY.

THREEPIO: How rude. It withdrew without even saying good day. *(OVER NEXT)* I don't think they're going to let us in, Artoo. We'd better go—["—and report this to Master Luke."] *(REACTING TO NEXT)* Eh?

Sound: Massive bolts slide back, unlocking the gate. Metallic echoes boom. Heavy motors, gears grinding, the portal scraping in its track as it's raised, under next.

THREEPIO: They're raising the portal. My goodness, it's dark in there, isn't it?

ARTOO: NATTERS BRIEFLY, OVER NEXT.

Sound: Artoo gets into motion, treads and motors revving, etc., moving off, under next.

THREEPIO: Artoo, wait. We're here for delicate negotiations. I really don't think we should rush into all this.

ARTOO: BUZZES, "LEAD, FOLLOW, OR GET OUTTA THE WAY," MOVING OFF.

THREEPIO: *(MOVING OFF)* Artoo, this is no time to be impetuous!

Sound: Scene fades.

SCENE 1–5   THE VAULTED ENTRANCE AREA OF JABBA'S FRONT GATE

Sound: Echoing, dripping—sand-winds from off.

THREEPIO: Gracious, it's like a darkened tomb in here.

ARTOO: TONES UNCERTAINLY.

THREEPIO: *(OVER NEXT)* Wait, what was that?

GAMORREANS #1 & #2: SNUFFLING, GRUNTING MENAC-INGLY, MOVING ON.

THREEPIO: Gamorrean guards. It would have to be those dis-gusting green ruffians.

ARTOO: BLAAATS HIS OPINION OF GAMORREANS.

THREEPIO: Just you deliver Master Luke's message so that we can get out of here. *(REACTING TO NEXT)* Oh my!

Sound: The huge armored portal is lowered again to bolt shut, under next.

THREEPIO: They're closing the portal again!

ARTOO: ALERTS THREEPIO, HAVING SPOTTED BIB FORTUNA APPROACHING.

THREEPIO: Twi'lek? What Twi'lek? *(OVER NEXT)* Where—oh!

Sound: Bib Fortuna's slippers scuffing on the stone floor, drawing near.

BIB FORTUNA: <Tay chuda, musuq!>

THREEPIO: Yes, I realize we have arrived uninvited, sir. I presume you to be Bib Fortuna, majordomo to Jabba the Hutt? I was told I would recognize you by your, that is, your magnificent cranial tentacles—

BIB FORTUNA: <Die Wanna Wanga!>

THREEPIO: Dear me, er . . . <Die Wanna Waugow.> We bring a message for your master.

BIB FORTUNA: <Die Jabba wanga?>

ARTOO: LETS OUT A STRING OF QUICK SOUND SYNTH.

THREEPIO:—that's right, Artoo, "and a gift." *(BEAT)* "Gift?" . . . What "gift?"

BIB FORTUNA: <Nee Jabba no badda.> *(TO ARTOO, CAJOLINGLY)* <Ees eye oh toe, Artoo Detoowha.>

ARTOO: REACTING TO BIB FORTUNA'S BLANDISHMENTS, GIGGLES AND TITTERS.

THREEPIO: Give you the gift and the message? I'm not sure if our master would approve of such a procedure.

12

ARTOO: AGREES PRIMLY.

THREEPIO: My counterpart says that our instructions are to give these things only to Jabba himself. In person.

BIB FORTUNA: <Zee chada oh mootee. Me chaade su goodie.>

THREEPIO: I'm terribly sorry. Artoo is ever so stubborn about this sort of thing.

BIB FORTUNA: *(OFFENDED)* <Nudd Chaa.> *(MOVING OFF)* <Nudd Chaa, Totonno.>

THREEPIO: *(TO BIB FORTUNA, AS THREEPIO MOVES OFF)* Jabba's audience chamber is that way? Thank you; thank you so much, sir. *(TO ARTOO)* Come along, Artoo.

ARTOO: PEEPS A ROGER-WILCO.

Sound: Artoo whirrs into motion, moves off, under next.

THREEPIO: *(MOVING OFF)* . . . Artoo, I have a bad feeling about this . . .

Sound: Hallway fades.

SCENE 1–6   JABBA'S MAIN AUDIENCE CHAMBER

Sound: "Aubade" music, in the background, from Max Rebo's band. Socializing and startup-phase carousing. Drinking vessels clinking. Laughter and peripheral buzz, much of it from nonhumans. Alien languages.

THREEPIO: My stars, what an appalling scene!

ARTOO: BLURTS AN INQUIRY.

THREEPIO: No, Artoo, I have never seen a more sinister and depraved crowd. One would think the rest of the galaxy safe, what with every thug, debaucher, and scofflaw having gathered here.

ARTOO: WARBLES A QUESTION.

THREEPIO: Well, yes, Jabba the Hutt would be that huge, sluglike individual on the dais, but I do not recommend you address him that way.

BIB FORTUNA: *(OFF, BY JABBA'S SIDE)* <Jabba, kada no pase mylota.>

JABBA: *(FROM OFF)* <O-oooo, Uuuu-mmmmm.>

THREEPIO: *(TO OFF)* Jabba. *(INDICATING MOVEMENT)* Coming, sir—coming.

JABBA: *(CLOSER TO THREEPIO'S POV NOW)* <Bo Shuda!> *(SNORTS, RUMBLES, SMACKS HIS LIPS)*

THREEPIO: Good morning . . . Your Magnitude. Artoo, play Master Luke's message for our host.

ARTOO: A QUICK ELECTRONIC BIRDSONG OF RESPONSE.

Sound: Activation noises and static as Artoo switches on his holoprojection function, as with the Princess Leia holo in "A New Hope."

LUKE: *(VIA HOLORECORDING)* Greetings, Exalted One. Allow me to introduce myself. I am Luke Skywalker—Jedi Knight, and friend to Captain Solo.

JABBA: <Oooo-oo.>

LUKE: I know you are powerful, mighty Jabba, and that your anger with Solo must be equally powerful. I seek an audience with Your Greatness to bargain for Solo's life.

JABBA: <Ho-ho-ho; Waw-haw-haw!>

CROWD: LAUGHTER AND CATCALLS, BACKGROUND.

SALACIOUS CRUMB: *(FROM OFF)* A MANIACAL CACKLE.

LUKE: *(OVER LAST PART OF PRECEDING REACTIONS)* With your wisdom, I'm sure that we can work out an arrangement which will be mutually beneficial and enable us to avoid any unpleasant confrontation. As a token of my goodwill, I present to you a gift: these two droids, Artoo-Detoo and See-Threepio.

THREEPIO: What did he say?

LUKE: Both are hardworking and will serve you well. I await your decision.

Sound: Static stops. Artoo's holo function switches off.

THREEPIO: This can't be! Artoo, you played the wrong message!

ARTOO: CHIRPS OFFENDEDLY.

BIB FORTUNA: <Jabba, mahstah fahgan etwor not, yees no Jedi!>

JABBA: <Ha, ono wangee gogh pah ool!> *(CHORTLES EVILLY)*

THREEPIO: "There will be no bargain?" We're doomed!

JABBA: <Peecha wangee cogh pah. Tong nam nee took chan kee troi, ho-ho!>

THREEPIO: Jabba declares that he will not give up his favorite wall decoration. He says that he likes Captain Solo where he is. Artoo, look! It's Captain Solo, still frozen in a slab of carbonite!

ARTOO: CHITTERS HIS DISTRESS.

JABBA: *(CHORTLES AGAIN)*

CROWD: JOIN IN, BACKGROUND.

CRUMB: SHRIEKS WITH GLEE.

JABBA: <Maypin ti yanki hequay!>

THREEPIO: Now Jabba's ordering them to take us into service. We are to be his slaves.

ARTOO: FIZZLES HIS MISGIVING.

GAMORREANS #1 & #2: SNUFFLING, OINKING, AS THEY APPROACH TO HEM IN THE TWO DROIDS AND HERD THEM AWAY, UNDER NEXT.

THREEPIO: Oh oh! There's no need for violence.

ARTOO: TONES AND BUZZES PUGNACIOUSLY.

THREEPIO: Artoo, kindly do not agitate the Gamorreans! *(TO GAMORREANS)* We will come quietly. *(TO HIMSELF)* Oh dear . . .

Sound: Main audience chamber fades.

SCENE 1–7   JABBA'S DUNGEONS

Sound: Echoes and the drip of water, cries, wild lines, and jabbers from crazed, caged prisoners. Sound of a rattling hoosegow door slamming shut, off, having admitted the droids and their guard.

THREEPIO: *(MOVING ON)* All right, I'm going. There's no need to shove.

GAMORREAN #1: *(MOVING ON)* HUFFING AND HARASSING.

THREEPIO: Artoo! Stay close!

ARTOO: CLUCKS UNHAPPILY.

THREEPIO: Sent to the dungeons! What could possibly have come over our master? Could it be something I did? He never expressed any unhappiness with my work.

ARTOO: CLAIMS TO BE MYSTIFIED.

THREEPIO: Our hour has come. We will never leave this dank netherworld in one piece.

GAMORREAN #1: CHIVVIES HIM TO MOVE ALONG, UNDER NEXT.

THREEPIO: Yes, yes, I'm going. Where, through that door? Very well, since resistance is useless . . .

Sound: Dungeon corridor fades.

SCENE 1–8   DUNGEON MACHINE SHOP

Sound: Racket of equipment, hum and pop of plasma torches, metallic hammering. Lasers cutting alloy. The various audible commo signals of diverse automata. The whirrs and whines of their servos. Creak of metal being bent, hiss of venting steam and skirling of drills.

THREEPIO: Mercy, it's something out of a droid's nightmare. Look, Artoo: they're branding the soles of that poor little power droid's feet!

Sound: Torture apparatus cranks, turning the 'bot upside down. Power droid gives out mouselike squeals of fear. Hissing and searing noises, as the red-hot thermal elements press into the power droid's soles, under next.

POWER DROID: CRIES OUT IN AGONY.

THREEPIO: May the maker preserve us!

NINEDENINE: *(COLD, CLIPPED VOICE ALTHOUGH NINEDENINE*

IS A FEMALE DROID) What have we here? You are a protocol droid, are you not?

THREEPIO: I am See-Threepio, human cy—

NINEDENINE: Yes or no will do.

THREEPIO: In that case, "yes" . . .

NINEDENINE: How many languages do you speak?

THREEPIO: I am fluent in over six million forms of communication and can readily—

NINEDENINE: Splendid. We have been without an interpreter since Jabba got angry with our last one and disintegrated him.

THREEPIO: Disintegrated?

NINEDENINE: Other units he melts, or feeds into the grinder unit. Guard, this protocol droid might be useful . . . temporarily. Fit him with a restraining bolt and take him back up to His Excellency's main audience chamber.

GAMORREAN #1: SNURFLES AND CHUGS, TAKING THREE-PIO'S ARM AND DRAGGING HIM OFF.

THREEPIO: *(REACTS, MOVING OFF)* Artoo, Don't forsake me! Oh-hh!

ARTOO: WARBLES AN ENCOURAGEMENT TO THREEPIO.

NINEDENINE: You're a feisty little one.

ARTOO: BRISTLES AT HER.

NINEDENINE: But you'll soon learn respect. I have need for an R2 unit on Jabba's sail barge. You'll fill in nicely. Or else.

ARTOO: LETS OUT A DUBIOUS SIMPER.

Sound: Dungeon fades.

SCENE 1–9A   JABBA'S MAIN AUDIENCE CHAMBER

Sound: Audience chamber comes up, this time in an advanced state of licentiousness. Quarrels, innuendo, libertinism in background—much of it in alien languages.

Music: Max Rebo's band playing Oola's dance number.

THREEPIO: This restraining bolt will cause me to short-circuit before long, if I'm not trampled by one of these ruffians first. Oh, my! There's Boba Fett! Oh, what am I doing here? I'm sure I don't deserve such a horrible fate. I wish Artoo were here. He's much better suited to this madness than I am. *(REACTS AS HE BUMPS INTO ARICA)* Oh! Excuse me!

ARICA: Watch where you're stepping!

THREEPIO: I am terribly sorry, madam. All of this boisterous behavior has quite upset my equilibrium. I see you are a dancing girl. I had no idea Jabba employed quite so many.

ARICA: I'm his latest acquisition. I've heard the girls make a lot of money dancing here. At least, the ones that survive till payday.

THREEPIO: Well, I hope your salary is more generous than your costume, Miss . . . ?

ARICA: You can call me Arica.

THREEPIO: And I am See-Threepio, human-cyborg relations.

ARICA: I saw the show you and that R2 unit put on. You used to belong to someone named Skywalker?

THREEPIO: Indeed, and I'm quite sure there's been a grave mistake. Master Luke would never abandon me to this den of thieves. At least, I hope not.

ARICA: So you think Skywalker really will come for you?

JABBA: *(LAUGHING AND CALLING OUT TO OOLA THE DANCER, OFF)* <Da Eitha!>

THREEPIO: Oh, now what?

ARICA: Jabba's calling on one of his dancers. That's Oola. If you've never seen a Twi'lek female dance, you're in for a treat.

THREEPIO: Yes, she's quite flexible.

JABBA: *(OFF, AND A BIT ANGRIER)* <Da Eitha!>

ARICA: She's Jabba's current favorite.

THREEPIO: I suppose that must be why he keeps her chained to his throne.

ARICA: It won't last. There's one dance she won't do for Jabba, no matter how much he pays her.

JABBA: *(OFF)* <Tua Utta Jabba?>

Sound: Rattle of the chain as Jabba yanks Oola closer to him, off.

THREEPIO: Oh, my! He's dragging her toward him by the chain! She won't have much choice now, I'm afraid.

Sound: More chain rattling.

ARICA: She's putting up a good fight. From what I know of Jabba, he won't tolerate that for long.

Sound: Music halts.

JABBA: <Boscka!>

Sound: A thump as Jabba's fist slams the trapdoor control. Trapdoor drops open, under next.

THREEPIO: He's activated some sort of trapdoor! That poor girl is falling in!

OOLA: SCREAMS AS SHE FALLS INTO THE RANCOR PIT, HER

RECEDING VOICE MINGLING WITH THE DISTANT, MUFFLED ROAR OF THE RANCOR. JABBA'S COURT CHEERS AND JEERS.

THREEPIO: Is that a rancor? How horrid! Won't somebody help her, Arica? *(REALIZES SHE'S VANISHED)* Arica? Where has she got to? Oh, I can't look!

OOLA: SCREAMS RISE IN TERROR, THEN CUT OFF ABRUPTLY DURING NEXT.

Sound: (Off) The rancor roars savagely as it grabs Oola. Sound of it chomping down on her.

THREEPIO: Oh, that poor, poor, creature.

SCENE 1–9B JABBA'S MAIN AUDIENCE CHAMBER

CROWD: REACTS TO GUNFIRE WITH VARIOUS HUMAN AND NONHUMAN EXCLAMATIONS.

THREEPIO: Someone's shooting!

JABBA: <Owouhhh? Kahjee tah, droid!>

THREEPIO: *(INDICATING MOVEMENT)* I'm right here, Your Enormity! *(TO THE ROOM AT LARGE)* Master Jabba demands to know who fired a weapon.

BOUSHH (LEIA): *(VOICE PROCESSED IN SCRATCHY MONO-TONE TO DENOTE HELMET)* <Eyah-tay, eyah-tay. Boushh, yo-toe.>

THREEPIO: O preeminent Jabba, this interloper says he is the bounty hunter Boushh. He states that . . . he has come for the bounty on this Wookiee, whom he brings before you in chains!

Sound: Chewbacca rattling manacles and leg irons, off.

CHEWBACCA: *(FROM OFF)* ROARS UNHAPPILY.

THREEPIO: Oh no! Chewbacca!

JABBA: *(LAUGHS NASTILY)* <Cheesa eejah wahkee Chewbahkah!>

THREEPIO: Jabba proclaims, "At last we have the mighty Chewbacca."

CHEWBACCA: MAKES A KEENING SOUND.

JABBA: <Yu-bahk ko rahto kama wahl bahk? Eye yees ka cho. Kawa Woo-kee.>

THREEPIO: The illustrious Jabba bids you welcome, Boushh, and will gladly pay you the reward of twenty-five thousand.

BOUSHH: <Yo-toe, yo-toe.>

THREEPIO: Boushh demands fifty thousand. No less.

JABBA: <Koto bossa feety hahto?> *(BELLOWS LIKE AN ANGRY SEA ELEPHANT)*

THREEPIO: Please, Master! I'm only translating—*(INDICATING IMPACT AS JABBA STRIKES HIM AND MOVEMENT AS HE'S KNOCKED TO THE FLOOR, OVER NEXT)* Ah-hh!

Sound: Threepio clatters from the throne dais to the throne room floor.

THREEPIO: But . . . Your Voluminousness, why be angry with me?

JABBA: <Moonon keejo? Eye!>

THREEPIO: The mighty Jabba asks Boushh why Jabba must pay fifty thousand.

BOUSHH: <Ay. Yo-toe.> *(OVER NEXT)*

Sound: Clicking as Boushh/Leia shows the thermal detonator and begins priming it.

THREEPIO: Boushh demands it . . . because he's holding a thermal detonator!

Sound: A loud click as Boushh arms the detonator, and a series of quickening pings or bleeps, indicating that it's counting down.

CROWD: YOWLS AND INTERJECTIONS AS THEY PANIC. SALACIOUS CRUMB'S DERANGED CACKLING IS PART OF IT, UNDER NEXT.

JABBA: *(LAUGHS BOOMINGLY)* <Kaso ya yee koli tra do kahn nee go. Yu bahn chuna leepa.>

THREEPIO: The Awesome Jabba says that this bounty hunter is his kind of scum: fearless and inventive.

JABBA: <Kuo meeta tah te fye. Dah tee teema nye.>

THREEPIO: The Magnanimous Jabba therefore offers the sum of thirty-five thousand. And I do suggest you take it, Boushh.

BOUSHH: <Ya-toe. Cha.>

THREEPIO: He agrees!

Sound: Boushh releases a switch on the detonator. Bleeping countdown stops.

CROWD: SIGHS OF RELIEF AND CHEERS.

CRUMB: HYSTERICAL LAUGHTER.

Sound: The partying resumes. Band strikes up again.

JABBA: <Kikin hamuspa Woo-kee chupa kiru.>

THREEPIO: The Exalted Jabba commands that Chewbacca be taken to the dungeons.

CHEWBACCA: *(OFF)* LOWS MOURNFULLY, OVER NEXT.

Sound: Wrist binders rattling and chains clinking as guards take him off.

CHEWBACCA: LAMENTS, MOVING COMPLETELY OFF.

THREEPIO: *(TO HIMSELF)* More's the pity.

CROWD: JEERS AND CATCALLS.

Sound: Scene fades.

SCENE 1–10A MAIN AUDIENCE CHAMBER, LATE NIGHT

Sound: The quiet of postcarousal nighttime at Jabba's. Snores and rhythmic or cyclical sound in the background. Alien snoozing, somnolent rumblings, coma respirations, etc.

BIB FORTUNA: *(A STAGE WHISPER)* <Eese teh, Seethreepiowha!>

Sound: Bib Fortuna thumbs a switch on the control unit of Threepio's restraining bolt.

THREEPIO: *(MOVING ON)* Ouch! Majordomo Fortuna. It truly wasn't necessary to excruciate my circuits with the restraining-bolt activator!

BIB FORTUNA: <Manta payra wasi. Shhh!>

THREEPIO: *(STAGE WHISPER)* But why are we all hiding back here behind the curtain?

JABBA: *(STAGE WHISPER)* <Iskay khuchu pach gogh.> *(LAUGHS CRAFTILY)*

THREEPIO: A surprise, Master Jabba? Why, how . . . jolly . . .

Sound: (Off) A door slides open and Boushh/Leia's footsteps move into middle off.

THREEPIO: It's that bounty hunter, Boushh.

BIB FORTUNA: Shhhh!

Sound: (Middle off) Boushh/Leia moves to the carbonite slab, releases a lever to lower the slab to the floor with a boom.

THREEPIO: But why is Boushh tampering with Captain Solo's carbonite slab?

24

Sound: Boushh/Leia begins throwing switches etc. to unfreeze Han.

THREEPIO: And why would he activate the mechanism to thaw Captain Solo?

Sound: The slab's defrost cycle boots up, disassembling the carbonite slab's molecules around Han and restarting his life functions, under next.

THREEPIO: The carbonite is melting! His hands are moving . . . It's working. Captain Solo survived! He's alive!

HAN: *(MIDDLE OFF, GROANS AS HE'S FREED UP FROM THE SOLO-SHAPED NICHE IN THE SLAB. SHIVERING WITH REACTION, AFTER-EFFECTS, ETC.)* Let me out! Get me out of this thing! *(SHIVERS AS HE SPEAKS)* What's happened to me?

Sound: Han collapses to the floor, under next.

BOUSHH: No, don't try to stand up yet. Just relax for a moment. I freed you from the carbonite.

HAN: Something's wrong . . .

BOUSHH: You have hibernation sickness.

HAN: I can't see.

BOUSHH: Your eyesight will return in time.

HAN: Where am I?

BOUSHH: In Jabba's palace.

Sound: Han fumbling to identify his rescuer by touch, only to find the helmet face bowl and mouth grill.

HAN: Why're you hiding behind that helmet? Why'd you de-ice me? Who are you?

SCENE 1–10B   MAIN AUDIENCE CHAMBER, LATE NIGHT

Sound: Clicks and the creak of the helmet's leather and metal, as Boushh/Leia removes it.

BOUSHH/LEIA: *(NOW REVEALED AS LEIA)* Someone who loves you, Han.

HAN: Leia! . . . *(INDICATES HER KISSING HIM)*

LEIA: *(BREAKS OFF THE KISS)* Save your strength, Han. I've got to get you out of here. Are you strong enough to stand up? *(INDICATES EFFORT OF HELPING HIM UP AND OF GETTING TO HER OWN FEET, WITH NEXT)*

HAN: *(INDICATING EFFORT OF STANDING, IN WEAKENED CONDITION)* Yeah, if it'll get me out of that big slug's filthy wallow.

JABBA: LAUGHS OUT LOUD.

HAN: I know that laugh.

JABBA: <Oo tay ah go day wah. Ko jay mada.>

THREEPIO: *(TO LACKIES, OFF)* The Prestidigitory Jabba commands that the curtain be opened!

Sound: Some humming/drapery as the curtain is raised.

HAN: Jabba.

LEIA: *(CONFIRMING IT FOR SIGHTLESS HAN)* Jabba, Boba Fett—the whole sick crew, Han.

HAN: Jabba, look, I was just on my way to pay you back when I got a little sidetracked. It's not my fault.

JABBA: *(LAUGHS)* <Ah chee ka gogh. Yu nee, Solo. Uu na keeng saleen na bach bahdlah beeska chatah, wee now kong "bantha pudu.">

26

HAN: This'll be bad for business, Jabba. Look, why can't we—sit down and straighten it all out?

JABBA: <Ya tha meen chool.>

THREEPIO: The dungeons, sir! No!

HAN: Jabba, I'll pay you triple.

GAMORREANS #1 & #2: SNURFLE AND SALIVATE AS THEY GRAB HAN.

HAN: (INDICATING RESISTANCE) Lemme go! (TO JABBA) Jabba, you're throwing away a fortune!

GAMORREANS #1 & #2: OINK, ETC., AS THEY DRAG HIM COMPLETELY OFF, UNDER NEXT.

HAN: Don't be a fool, Jabba! I'm on the level this time!

JABBA: <Rah toe! Co slayats my.> (CHUCKLES PRURIENTLY)

THREEPIO: Jabba further commands that the Princess Leia be brought to him.

Sound: More Gamorrean huffing and puffing, moving on as other guards drag the princess to Jabba and Threepio's pov, under next.

LEIA: (INDICATES BEING SEIZED, FROG-MARCHED TO JABBA) (MOVING ON) I'm warning you, Jabba! We have powerful friends. You're going to regret this.

JABBA: <Oolo tah. Ah nah mah toe tah. Eyah!>

THREEPIO: The, er, Voluptuary Jabba is unworried. He observes that the Princess Leia Organa looks, that is, good enough to eat.

JABBA: LAUGHS SLYLY.

CROWD: REGISTER THEIR GLEE AT HER PREDICAMENT.

CRUMB: GIVES OUT A CACHINNATING LAUGH.

Sound: Jabba's big wet anaconda tongue, as it comes slithering stickily out to take a taste of Leia, under next.

LEIA: Get that tongue off me, you repulsive Hutt degenerate—*(AS HE GETS HIS LICKS IN)* Ugh!

JABBA: BOOMS WITH GLEE.

CRUMB: SHRIEKS WITH AMUSEMENT.

THREEPIO: I can't bear to watch. Woe is us! How could Master Luke allow it to come to this? It's the end of us all . . .

Sound: Jabba's main audience chamber fades.

NARRATOR: The Rebels haven't known so dire a moment since the disaster at Cloud City. But out on the endless dunes of Tatooine, a lone figure walks: one solitary unarmed knight, moving inexorably toward an appointed reckoning in the palace of Jabba the Hutt.

Music: Closing theme up under credits.

NARRATOR: CLOSING CREDITS.

EPISODE TWO:

"FAST FRIENDS"

CAST:
Han
Boba Fett
Jabba the Hutt
Lando
Leia
Luke
Bib Fortuna
Threepio
Skiff Guards
Sail Barge Guards
Barada

SOUND/FX ROLES:
Chewbacca
Gamorrean #1
Gamorrean #2
Rancor
Artoo-Detoo
Sarlaac
Salacious Crumb

ANNOUNCER: OPENING CREDITS.

Music: Opening theme.

NARRATOR: A long time ago in a galaxy far, far away there came a time of revolution, when Rebels united to challenge a tyrannical Empire. Now the Empire is pressing hard to complete a second Death Star, a planet-destroying battle station intended to crush the Rebel Alliance once and for all. But on the desert planet of Tatooine, more immediate disaster looms for the key members of the Rebel leadership. In a grim fortress-palace, Princess Leia, Han Solo, and Chewbacca the Wookiee are prisoners of the vile gangster, Jabba the Hutt. The droids See-Threepio and Artoo-Detoo, sent to Jabba as gifts by Luke Skywalker, are powerless to help. Though Leia has managed to thaw Han from the carbonite slab in which he was imprisoned, he has emerged blinded by hibernation sickness. And as the princess becomes a captive plaything of the evil Jabba, Han is being dragged to dungeons deep under the palace.

SCENE 2–1   JABBA'S DUNGEONS

Sound: Echoing; dripping water, in the background. Howls, wild lines, and yammering of human and nonhuman prisoners. Cellblock door rolls shut, off.

HAN: *(INDICATING EFFORT AND THE SHIVERING, ETC., OF HIBERNATION SICKNESS; MOVING ON)* Hey, watch the shovin'. I said lay off, ya stinkin', flat-nosed Gamorrean boneheads.

GAMORREANS #1 & #2: *(MOVING ON)* CHUFF AND GRUNT, HUSTLING HIM ALONG.

HAN: Real brave against a guy who can't see, aren't cha? When my eyes come back on-line I'm gonna find you, rip your horns out, and use 'em for coat hooks.

Sound: Cell door opens.

HAN: Oh, my new accommodations, huh? The Imperial suite?

GAMORREANS #1 & #2: WHUFFLE AND SLOBBER AS THEY SHOVE HIM INSIDE.

HAN: *(INDICATES BEING PUSHED)* Ya drooling slobs.

Sound: Cell door clinks shut, under next.

HAN: Your mother's a set of matched luggage! *(SNIFFS THE AIR EXPERIMENTALLY)* Whew! Yeah, smells like a prison cell, all right.

Sound: Chewbacca stirs off, under next.

CHEWBACCA: GROWLS WARNINGLY, OFF, NOT YET AWARE WHO HAN IS.

HAN: Who's that? Who's there?

CHEWBACCA: A BARK OF RECOGNITION.

HAN: Chewie, is that you? Chewie!

CHEWBACCA: *(MOVING ON)* YOWLS AND BLEATS IN EXCITE-MENT, OVER NEXT.

Sound: Chewbacca grabs and pats Han in reunion.

HAN: *(INDICATING THE IMPACT)* Wait, I can't see, pal. What's goin' on?

CHEWBACCA: RATTLES OFF AN EXPOSITORY STRING OF YIPS, HOOTS, AND ROARS.

HAN: Luke? Luke's crazy. He can't even take care of himself, much less rescue us.

CHEWBACCA: GROWLS INSISTENTLY.

HAN: He says he's a Jedi Knight? Oh, great! Leia tried to be a one-princess rescue team and now Jabba's got her. I'm out of it for a little while and everybody's having delusions of grandeur.

CHEWBACCA: WOOOS AND UURRRRRS.

HAN: What d'ya mean "Lando's here, too?" Chewie, I need you— don't start hallucinating on me.

CHEWBACCA: WOOFS OFFENDEDLY.

HAN: Okay, okay, don't get your fur all ruffled.

CHEWBACCA: YAWPS AFFECTIONATELY AS HE HUGS HAN.

HAN: *(INDICATES THE POWER OF A WOOKIEE SQUEEZE)* Oof! Yeah, I love you, too. Only, go easy with the hugs, huh? Cracked ribs are a problem I can do without right now.

CHEWBACCA: RUMBLES HIS CONCERN.

HAN: I'm all right, pal.

Sound: Han pats Chewbacca comfortingly.

HAN: I'm all right.

Sound: Footsteps indicate Boba Fett's approach.

HAN: What's that? Who's there?

CHEWBACCA: GIVES A LOW, HATEFUL GROWL.

HAN: Boba Fett? I was just saying the stench couldn't get any worse, Fett, and you show up to make a liar out of me. *(SHORT PAUSE. BOBA FETT DOES NOT TAKE HIS BAIT)* What're you doing down here? Jabba got you scrubbing floors in your spare time? Or have you worked up the guts to shoot it out while I'm still half-frozen?

CHEWBACCA: BARKS HIS FRUSTRATION.

HAN: C'mon, bounty hunter, you didn't come here just to stare!

FETT: I've beaten you, Solo.

HAN: Beaten me? You? Vader captured us. Jabba's got us. All you did was fetch and carry.

FETT: Tomorrow I'll collect another bounty. And you'll be dead.

HAN: I've bargained with Jabba before—don't worry about me. What about you—you still Jabba's little errand boy?

FETT: Watch your mouth, Solo. I risked my tail to get you here.

CHEWBACCA: A ROLLING, SARCASTIC GROWL.

HAN: Yeah, Chewie, I think you're right. We struck a nerve. I'll bet he's not as cocky as he wants people to think. In fact, he sounds just a little nervous to me. Are you nervous, Fett? Worried that we'll get out of this hole and track you down?

FETT: *(LAUGHS)* I'm going to enjoy watching you die.

Sound: Scuffle of boots, then slow, steady footsteps recede, under next.

HAN: *(SHOUTING AFTER HIM)* You think a little thing like death's gonna slow us down? You'd better be looking over your shoulder, bounty hunter. 'Cause sooner or later we'll find you! I'm gonna rip your helmet off with your head inside!

SCENE 2-2 JABBA'S MAIN AUDIENCE CHAMBER

Sound: Room comes up in the quiet downtime of early morning. Perhaps some soft music, but the socializing is very muted after the excesses and action of preceding events. Presume it to be A.M. following Leia's capture and Han's defrost. There are a few stirring automatons, alien snores again, etc. Jabba's snoozing.

LANDO: *(STAGE WHISPER, FROM SLIGHTLY OFF)* Leia! Leia! Your Highness!

LEIA: *(STAGE WHISPER)* Who's—Lando!

LANDO: *(MOVING ON)* No, Lando Calrissian wouldn't last long in Jabba the Hutt's main audience chamber, Princess. Here, I am merely Tamtel. Tamtel Skreej, a humble guard from one of Jabba's sand skiffs.

LEIA: I see . . . "Tamtel."

LANDO: Are you all right?

LEIA: Yes, but this slave outfit isn't exactly warm. And the chain pinches and the collar chafes.

LANDO: The old saying's right, Leia: Beauty can be a curse.

LEIA: So gallant. You'd flirt with your own executioner if she were a woman.

LANDO: Especially her. I might persuade her to botch the job. But I'm afraid there's not much I can do for you. We don't dare risk another play until Luke gets here.

LEIA: He'd better make it soon. My dancing's not so good. If I have to perform for Jabba I'm gonna end up in the rancor pit a lot faster than Oola did.

LANDO: I hope Luke knows what he's doing, because things are getting hairier than a Wookiee around here.

SCENE 2–3 JABBA'S PALACE ENTRY AREA INTERIOR

Sound: Entrance area comes up. Gamorrean guards, distant humming of machinery, echoes, etc. Marching footsteps of guard detachment moving off. The massive, armored front portal unlocks suddenly and without warning.

GAMORREANS #1 & #2: REACT IN SURPRISE AND ALARM.

Sound: The portal is raised by its brute motor, racheting, etc., creaking and groaning in its track. Chain rattling.

GAMORREANS #1 & #2: THEY'RE EVEN MORE EDGY AND HOSTILE.

Sound: Door stops. Tatooine winds heard, off. Luke's unhurried footsteps, moving on.

GAMORREANS #1 & #2: WHUFFLES EXCITEDLY.

LUKE: *(MOVING ON)* Don't be afraid, guards. I'm not here to do harm.

GAMORREANS #1 & #2: PUZZLE AND BOGGLE AMONG THEMSELVES.

LUKE: Lower your weapons, and move aside.

Sound: Gamorreans' axe-weapons clank and ring as the blades barring Luke's way are lowered.

LUKE: *(MORE STERNLY)* Let me by, I say.

GAMORREANS #1 & #2: FALL BACK TO EITHER SIDE, CHOKING AND GASPING.

LUKE: That's better. Your breath will come back to you in a moment. There's no need to raise the alarm. *(MOVING OFF)* I can find my own way to Jabba's audience chamber.

GAMORREANS #1 & #2: MURMUR BETWEEN THEMSELVES, NOT SURE WHAT JUST HAPPENED TO THEM.

SCENE 2–4A: JABBA'S MAIN AUDIENCE CHAMBER

Sound: The place is in an early-stage party phase. Max's band music, sound of crowd and drinking vessels—glass, etc.

JABBA: SNORTS, LAUGHS. *(BACKGROUND)*

BIB FORTUNA: <Yo mot tu cheep, do yo pan Skywalkah. Jabba mo baht toe baht too.>

LUKE: *(MOVING ON)* I know you to be Jabba's majordomo, Bib Fortuna. I must speak to your master.

BIB FORTUNA: <Shh. Ee toe seet. Jabba no two zand dehank obee. No pahgan.> ["no pahgan" = "no bargain."]

LUKE: You will take me to Jabba now.

BIB FORTUNA: *("ECHOING" LUKE'S INSTRUCTION)* <Et tu takku u Jabba now.>

LUKE: Good. You serve your master well.

BIB FORTUNA: <Eye sota va locha.>

LUKE: And you will be rewarded.

BIB FORTUNA: <Ba chu noya trot.> *(TO JABBA'S EAR)* <Mahstah Jabba. Gabba no pace Luke Skywalkah.>

THREEPIO: *(FROM OFF)* Master Luke! At last, Master Luke's come to rescue me!

LEIA: *(FROM OFF—NEAR JABBA'S POV BECAUSE SHE'S CHAINED TO HIS THRONE)* Luke! Luke, watch yourself.

LUKE: Don't worry, Leia. I'm just here to make Jabba see reason.

JABBA: <Ho-oo? Uuooomph? Seethreepiowha!>

Sound: Jabba smacks Threepio for catharsis and to get compliance on a translation. Suet hitting metal, etc.

THREEPIO: Ooww! Er, awaiting your orders, O Sublime Jabba.

JABBA: <Nah mass fa wong lee fah toon kay.>

THREEPIO: *(REACTING TO THE BLOW)* The, er, Preponderant Jabba gave specific orders not to admit Skywalker.

LUKE: *(INDICATING MOVEMENT AS HE APPROACHES JABBA)* I must be allowed to speak, Jabba.

BIB FORTUNA: <Jabba, Jedi modst be inco ee.>

JABBA: *(CLOSER TO LUKE'S POV NOW)* <Oowahhhh! Ko ja vaya sko. Ees turo na om Jedi mine chik.>

THREEPIO: Jabba berates Bib Fortuna for a weak-minded fool. He says, "Skywalker is using an old Jedi mind trick."

LUKE: Jabba, you will bring me Captain Solo and the Wookiee.

JABBA: <Oh-ho, ho ho, ho! Ya ku kacha ka puna ni sa. Ee?>

THREEPIO: The Impregnable Jabba says, "Your Jedi mind powers will not work on me, boy."

LUKE: Nevertheless, Jabba, I'm taking Captain Solo and his friends. You can either profit by this . . . or be destroyed. But I warn you not to underestimate my powers.

JABBA: <Ban gon wan she co, cach. O Jedi cho kanya wee shaja keecho.>

THREEPIO: The Unassailable Jabba replies, "There will be no bargain, young Jedi. I shall enjoy watching you die." He asks why you came to his home without a lightsaber with which to defend yourself.

LUKE: I'd hoped I wouldn't need weapons, Jabba. But a Jedi is never unarmed.

JABBA: <Whoa, ho, ho ho ho!>

THREEPIO: Master Luke, beware! You're standing on—["—a trapdoor that Jabba controls from his throne."]

JABBA: <Quotu manka ree tee jamutsa!>

LUKE: If you need to see me with a weapon, Jabba, will your guard's blaster do? I can call it from his hand to mine . . . like so—

Sound: A vibration, then some kind of chuff as the pistol's snatched from the Gamorrean's fist by Luke's Force powers. The blaster whizzes through the air, slaps into Luke's waiting—biosynergic prosthetic—hand.

GAMORREAN #1: REACTS TO PRECEDING, SQUEALING IN SURPRISE, ETC.

THREEPIO: *(OVER PRECEDING)* Well done, Master Luke!

LUKE: Jabba, do I have to use this thing or have you seen enough?

LEIA: Luke, there's another guard behind you!

GAMORREAN #2: FROTHS AND CHUGS, TRYING TO SUBDUE LUKE.

LUKE: REACTS, RESISTING THE GUARD.

LEIA: Get clear of him, Luke! You're standing on a trapdoor!

JABBA: <Boscka!> *(INDICATES MOTION OF SLAMMING HIS HAMMY FIST DOWN ON THE BUTTON)*

Sound: Jabba's fist thumps on the button, heavy click. Latches snick open and hinges creak, door bangs open under Luke's feet.

LUKE: REACTS TO THE FALL, GRUNTS FROM SUCCESSION OF IMPACTS AS HE TUMBLES DOWN THE CHUTE. POV FOLLOWS HIM.

SCENE 2–4B JABBA'S MAIN AUDIENCE CHAMBER

Sound: Luke kicking, jouncing as he falls. Same from Gamorrean #2.

GAMORREAN #2: SQUEALS AND SNORTS IN FEAR, SPIN-CYCLING DOWN THE CHUTE.

Sound: Sound environment "opens up" as Luke and Gamorrean #2 land tumbling on the sandy floor of the rancor's den.

LUKE: INDICATES LANDING, STRUGGLING TO HIS FEET.

GAMORREAN #2: THE SAME, PANTING FOR BREATH.

LEIA: *(OFF—FROM ABOVE THE PIT)* Luke! Are you all right?

LUKE: *(YELLING TO OFF)* Yeah, but a grating's blocking the chute. I can't get back up that way.

JABBA: *(OFF)* <Cheedee Jedi! Cheedee Jedi! Waw, haw-haw-haw-haw.>

THREEPIO: *(OFF)* Where is your blaster, Master Luke?

LUKE: Lost it on the way down. I don't see it anywhere.

Sound: Rumbling of rancor's cage door as it lifts, under next.

THREEPIO: Sir, you must get out of the pit before the rancor's cage door is opened.

LUKE: *(TO HIMSELF)* Too late for that.

GAMORREAN #2: MAKES FRANTIC SOUNDS, TERRIFIED AND SEEKING AN ESCAPE ROUTE.

LUKE: You! Guard! Stand over here with me. Our only chance is to take the rancor on together, hit-and-run.

GAMORREAN #2: PANICKED SOUNDS, AS HIS NERVE CRACKS.

RANCOR: LETS OUT A FEROCIOUS ROAR, MOVING ON.

GAMORREAN #2: SQUEALS IN HORROR, INDICATES EFFORT OF TRYING TO CLAMBER BACK UP CHUTE.

LUKE: Get back down here. The chute's blocked. You'll be cornered up there!

RANCOR: BELLOWS HUNGRILY AS IT GOES FOR THE GUARD.

LUKE: Hurry, it's seen you!

GAMORREAN #2: OINKS AND SCREECHES AS HE'S TAKEN.

Sound: Rancor grabs the Gamorrean guard and wolfs him down in a couple of chomps.

LUKE: *(TO RANCOR AND HIMSELF)* Hope that snack took the edge off your appetite, big fella.

RANCOR: A VORACIOUS GROWL.

LUKE: Guess not, huh?

LEIA: Luke, there's a club on that boulder behind you!

LUKE: *(TO HIMSELF)* Club? Mmm, a big legbone. Better than nothing, though.

THREEPIO: Beware, sir! The rancor is boxing you in!

LUKE: Yeah, no way to avoid him this time.

RANCOR: YOWLS.

THREEPIO: Master Luke, don't let him seize you—ohhh!

LUKE: *(INDICATING STRAIN OF BEING CLENCHED IN THE*

MONSTER'S CLAWS) Now that you've got me, what're you gonna do with me?

RANCOR: LICKS ITS CHOPS, SNARLING, PREPARING TO GOBBLE HIM.

LUKE: Let's see if you still feel hungry with this bone jammed in your craw! *(INDICATES EFFORT OF WEDGING THE BONE INTO THE RANCOR'S MOUTH)*

Sound: Splintering and squeaking as the beast's jaws exert pressure, bending the bone and snapping it, under next.

LUKE: *(INDICATES BEING DROPPED BY THE DISTRACTED RAN-COR)* Didn't . . . care for it, huh?

THREEPIO: Splendidly done, sir. You made him drop you!

LEIA: Luke, that door on the other side of the pit is your only way out.

LUKE: *(TO HIMSELF)* Maybe I can outflank him; there's no future in hanging around here. *(INDICATES EFFORT OF GATHERING HIMSELF, MAKING A DASH FOR IT)*

Sound: Luke's running footsteps.

RANCOR: TRUMPETS ANGRILY.

THREEPIO: Stay low, Master Luke, stay low!

Sound: Luke slams to a stop against the door.

LUKE: *(INDICATES IMPACT AS HE FETCHES UP AT THE DOOR)* Okay, c'mon, door . . .

Sound: Luke punching the control keyboard, door controls bleeping, under next.

LUKE: . . . open for me, baby . . .

Sound: Pneumatic hiss, whirr of machinery, as the "inner" door lifts—leaving the outer one still barring Luke's way.

42

LUKE: No!

LEIA: Luke, what is it?

LUKE: The outer door's still locked. I'm trapped.

THREEPIO: Sir, can you drop the holding-area portal?

LEIA: The controls are in a wall panel to your left.

RANCOR: GROWLS, STALKING LUKE AGAIN.

LUKE: *(TO HIMSELF AS WELL AS TO THE RANCOR)* Big boy, you're between me and those controls.

THREEPIO: Sir, if you threw something, it could trigger the portal release.

LEIA: Can you drop the portal, Luke?

LUKE: *(TO HIMSELF)* Maybe. Maybe I can drop it like the biggest deadweight trap on Tatooine.

RANCOR: SNARLS, CLOSING IN.

LUKE: Let's see . . . ahh. The skull of a previous dinner guest. This oughta do it.

THREEPIO: Sir, we can't see you. What is happening?

LUKE: One throw's all you're gonna get, Skywalker.

RANCOR: ROARS, LOOMING OVER HIM.

LUKE: C'mon . . . A little closer, that's it. Just where I want you!

RANCOR: HOWLS AT HIM.

LUKE: *(INDICATES EFFORT OF THROWING THE SKULL)*

Sound: Skull bonks control switch, near off. Crackle of short-circuit and small blast of a minor power system explosion, under next.

LUKE: Bull's-eye!

Sound: Portal releases and descends with a ground-shaking crash.

43

RANCOR: BAYS IN PAIN, THEN BREATHES ITS LAST.

THREEPIO: He's done it! He's slain the rancor!

LEIA: Luke, are you hurt?

LUKE: *(YELLING TO OFF)* So far, so good, Leia.

JABBA: *(OFF)* <Tootah! Ah-hhh! Oola loobah!>

THREEPIO: Jabba is most distraught.

JABBA: *(OFF)* <Yon tas Solo chung Wookiee ko lo yay man. Dabba kas no!>

THREEPIO: Sir, Jabba has ordered that Captain Solo and Chewbacca be brought before him to share in your punishment. I'm afraid he's highly incensed.

LUKE: *(TO HIMSELF)* Fine. That makes two of us.

SCENE 2–5   JABBA'S MAIN AUDIENCE CHAMBER

Sound: Ambient sounds. Footsteps of guards marching the prisoners in.

HAN: *(TO HIS GUARDS, MOVING ON)* Quit shovin', ya flat-nosed, pinheaded goon.

GAMORREAN #1: *(MOVING ON)* SNORTS A RESPONSE.

HAN: Just take the binders off us for two minutes, that's all we ask.

LUKE: *(TO SLIGHTLY OFF)* Han!

HAN: Luke!

LUKE: Are you two all right?

HAN: Fine. Right, Chewie?

CHEWBACCA: GIVES A GUTTURAL "NO SWEAT."

HAN: Except that somebody turned out the lights on me. Can't see a thing. So, here we are together again, huh?

LUKE: I just couldn't miss a party like this.

HAN: How are we doing?

LUKE: The same as always.

HAN: That bad, huh? Where's Leia?

LEIA: *(FROM SLIGHTLY OFF—JABBA'S THRONE)* I'm here, Han.

HAN: Look, thanks for trying to spring me, kid. You gave it your best.

JABBA: <Tak toy woo nee tong.>

THREEPIO: Oh dear. His High Exaltedness, the great Jabba the Hutt, has decreed that you are to be terminated immediately.

HAN: Good. I hate long waits.

THREEPIO: You will therefore be taken to the Dune Sea and cast into the Pit of Carkoon, nesting place of the all-powerful Sarlaac.

HAN: *(AN ASIDE)* That doesn't sound so bad.

THREEPIO: In the belly of the Great Abomination you will find a new definition of pain and suffering, as you are slowly digested over a thousand years!

LEIA: No!

HAN: On second thought, let's pass on it, huh?

LUKE: You should have bargained with me, Jabba.

JABBA: <Ya cha dee choo!>

LUKE: This is the last mistake you'll ever make.

JABBA: <Ho, ho, ho, waw-haw! My pek kikin Jedi sapa loy!>

THREEPIO: Jabba says, "And so—"

LUKE: I know. "And so dies the last of the Jedi." It's been said before, Jabba.

JABBA: *(ROARS ANGRILY)* <Keechay uru pacha saquay.>

THREEPIO: Jabba commands that the condemned be taken to the sand skiff, and that his sail barge be made ready for a voyage on the Dune Sea.

JABBA: <Reema cheeri huchu toota Jedi leek may.>

THREEPIO: Prepare a feast aboard Jabba's ship of the desert. Let great merriment attend the extermination of this, the last of the Jedi.

SCENE 2–6   INTERIOR, JABBA'S SAIL BARGE

Sound: Light sand-winds, off. Creak of the ironclad ship of the desert, its rigging singing and groaning, sails fluttering and snapping, etc. Max Rebo's band playing.

THREEPIO: *(MOVING ON, INDICATING THAT HE'S WENDING HIS WAY THROUGH A CROWD, ALSO INDICATING THAT THE VOYAGE HAS HIM SOMEWHAT SEASICK)* Excuse me, sir, I wonder if you mind getting off my foot for just a moment? . . . Coming through, there, with your permission, terribly sorr—[—"sorry, ladies and gentlemen."] Artoo!

ARTOO: TWEEDLES A GREETING.

THREEPIO: Artoo-Detoo! But—what are you doing here?

ARTOO: TWITTERS BACK AN ANSWER.

THREEPIO: Well I can see you're serving drinks—festooned with beverage dispensers like a vending machine. What have they done to you?

ARTOO: DEFENDS HIS ACTIONS.

THREEPIO: And look at me. The motion of this sail barge has upset my equilibrium sensors and I'm as seasick as a, a tauntaun in a typhoon.

ARTOO: MAINTAINS THAT EVERYTHING'S GOING TO WORK OUT.

THREEPIO: Hmm. I wish I had your confidence.

ARTOO: SHRUGS THAT IT'S ALL PART OF THE PLAN.

THREEPIO: "All part of the plan?" What plan? This is another of your fantasies, Artoo.

ARTOO: POO-POOS, "THAT'S HOW MUCH YOU KNOW."

THREEPIO: Look, over in that sand skiff: Poor, brave Master Luke bound and helpless, and Chewbacca and Captain Solo with him. All waiting to walk the plank.

ARTOO: LETS OUT A BURST.

THREEPIO: "Sarlaac off the starboard bow?" Where?

ARTOO: CLARIFIES.

THREEPIO: So that's the Pit of Carkoon?

JABBA: *(FROM OFF)* <Seethreepiowha, chap chay ahwa toe!>

THREEPIO: *(TO OFF)* Coming, O Most Festive Jabba. *(TO ARTOO)* I fear the moment of termination is at hand—wait, where are you running off to this time?

Sound: Artoo revs and moves out. Glasses, etc., clink as he goes.

ARTOO: REPLIES AS HE MOVES OFF.

THREEPIO: Take up your position on deck? Artoo, acting like a spy will get you thrown down the Sarlaac's maw, too!

JABBA: <Meel husk qwani Threepiowha!>

47

THREEPIO: *(TO SLIGHTLY OFF)* I'll be right there, Master Jabba! *(TO HIMSELF)* Alas, and rue the day. I'll be right there . . .

SCENE 2–7   OPEN DECK OF THE SAND SKIFF CARRYING THE CONDEMNED

Sound: More wind, fewer background voices. Creaking of iron plating. No sail sounds but perhaps a suspension/antigrav-field hum, engine vibration, etc.

HAN: Are we almost there, Luke? I'm getting real tired of waiting.

LUKE: Coming up on the Pit of Carkoon now, Han.

HAN: I think my eyes are getting better. Instead of a big dark blur, I see a big light blur.

LUKE: There's nothing much to see. I used to live here, y'know.

HAN: You're gonna die here, y'know. Convenient.

LUKE: Just stick close to Chewie and Lando. I've taken care of everything.

HAN: Oh, great.

BARADA: <Doe zan dun gustah, Chewbahccah!>

CHEWBACCA: GROWLS, HAVING BEEN SHOVED.

HAN: *(MOVING OFF)* Hey, lay off my partner.

BARADA: *(OFF)* <Iil go shood gah, Solo!>

LANDO: *(SOTTO VOCE)* Luke.

LUKE: *(SOTTO VOCE)* Careful, Lando. Don't draw their attention.

LANDO: Don't worry. Han's got the spotlight.

HAN: *(OFF)* Next one o' you vegetable-heads who touches us is gonna need prosthetics from the chin on down once we get our hands on ya!

CHEWBACCA: *(OFF)* BACKS THE THREAT WHOLEHEARTEDLY.

BARADA: *(LAUGHS AND JEERS, OFF)* <Muyu pukunah!>

LUKE: All set, Lando?

LANDO: Ready, but look out for Boba Fett. He's been watching us from the sail barge. He senses something's up.

LUKE: I can handle him. Look. Artoo's in position on the deck.

LANDO: I don't like waiting till the last second to make our move.

LUKE: They won't free my wrists until I'm out on the plank over the Sarlaac. That's when Jabba's guard will be down.

LANDO: You have an awful lot riding on one little astromech droid.

LUKE: It's not the first time.

Sound: The sand skiff's engines indicate it's decelerating and coming about.

HAN: *(MOVING ON)* Are we at the Sarlaac's nest? What d'you see?

LANDO: A great big funnel lined with teeth and tentacles, big enough to swallow this skiff whole.

BARADA: *(MOVING ON)* <Noka gogh vindi way!>

THREEPIO: *(FROM EXTRA OFF, OVER LOUDSPEAKER—ANY ECHOES WOULD BE OFF THE SAND SHIPS' SIDES, SINCE THE OPENNESS WOULD CARRY SOUND AWAY)* Victims of the Almighty Sarlaac! His Excellency hopes that you will die honorably. But should any of you wish to beg for mercy, the great Jabba the Hutt will now listen to your pleas.

BARADA & SKIFF GUARDS: *(FROM SLIGHTLY OFF)* CHUCKLE COARSELY AT THE SADISTIC HUMOR.

HAN: *(YELLS TO OFF)* Threepio, you can tell that slimy piece of worm-ridden filth he'll get no such pleasure from us. *(TO CHEW-BACCA)* Right, Chewie?

CHEWBACCA: SECONDS IT.

LUKE: *(YELLS TO OFF)* Jabba! This is your last chance. Free us or die.

JABBA: *(MALIGN LAUGHTER ROLLS ACROSS THE WAY FROM EX-TRA OFF)*

THREEPIO: Jabba commands that the plank be extended, and Skywalker moved into position.

BARADA: <Teeza lell chumpi quatta.>

LANDO: *(TO BARADA, OUT LOUD)* Yes, Barada. *(TO LUKE, SOTTO VOCE)* Prisoner, hold still while I remove your bonds.

HAN: This plan of yours, Luke. It does involve us not getting eaten, doesn't it?

LUKE: Stay back with Chewie, Han—unless you want to walk the plank before I do.

HAN: Hey, help yourself, shipmate.

LANDO: Prisoner, step to the end of the plank.

Sound: Luke's booted feet stepping out along the iron plank. Tatooine winds rise a little. Other background fades a little. Sound of the Sarlaac, off.

THREEPIO: *(FROM EXTRA OFF)* The Redoubtable Jabba commands, let Skywalker be cast into the Sarlaac.

LANDO: *(SOTTO VOCE)* Give Artoo the signal, Luke.

BARADA: <Kuchu wayway ees!>

HAN: Now or never, chum.

LUKE: Artoo!

ARTOO: TWEEDLES A RESPONSE FROM EXTRA OFF.

LUKE: *(YELLS)* Artoo—now!

ARTOO: ACKNOWLEDGES.

Sound: Extra off, Artoo's hidden receptacle has opened and raised Luke's concealed lightsaber into the open. Now it fires with a noise like a small pneumatic tube or mortar.

LUKE: INDICATES EFFORT AS HE STEPS OFF, GRABS THE EDGE OF THE PLANK ON HIS WAY DOWN, AND CATAPULTS HIMSELF BACK INTO THE AIR, SOMERSAULTING FOR THE SKIFF'S OPEN MAIN DECK.

Sound: The plank rebounds like a springboard as Luke's weight releases from it.

BARADA: <Waskha ees! Waskha ees!>

GUARDS: SHOUT IN SURPRISE AND APPREHENSION AS LUKE PLUNGES DOWN AMONG THEM.

LANDO: *(TO LUKE)* Heads up, Luke!

LUKE: Got it! *(INDICATES ACT OF CATCHING IT)*

HAN: What's going on, Lando?

LANDO: Luke's back aboard, Artoo's tossed him his lightsaber.

Sound: The lightsaber slaps into Luke's hand. Snap of a button as the blade ignites and flares to life.

HAN: I know that sound! Duck, Chewie! Heads're gonna roll now!

CHEWBACCA: HONKS AN ACKNOWLEDGMENT.

Sound: The lightsaber moans as it whirls, hitting Barada. Explosion of energy and tissue.

BARADA: GIVES A DEATH SCREAM THAT TRAILS OFF AS HE CRASHES THROUGH THE RAIL AND PLUNGES INTO THE SARLAAC.

LUKE: Lando, grab your axe, take the one in the bow!

LANDO: I'm on him. *(INDICATES THE EFFORT OF ENGAGING AN-OTHER GUARD AT CLOSE QUARTERS WITH THE AXE-BLADED "BAYONET" OF THE FIREARM HE'S CARRYING)*

Sound: The clang and clash of heavy, edged weapons. Luke's singing sword strikes again.

HAN: What's happening? Y'know, I'm still not getting a clear vi-sual, here.

LUKE: *(INDICATING EFFORT OF DEALING WITH ANOTHER GUARD)* We're a . . . little busy . . . Han!

Sound: More lightsaber war-song and dirge.

GUARD: LIKE BARADA, HE'S DRIVEN BACK OFF THE DECK, SCREAM TRAILING AWAY.

CHEWBACCA: A QUICK WARNING.

HAN: Chewie says the barge is getting ready to fire on us with a pivot gun!

LUKE: Turn around, Chewie. Let's get those ropes off you.

LANDO: *(INDICATES EFFORT OF EXCHANGING BLADE-STROKES WITH HIS OPPONENT, OFF)* Luke! Boba Fett's firing up that rocket pack! He'll be on us in a second.

LUKE: Let him come.

Sound: A blast from the sail barge deck gun strikes the skiff deck, off.

LANDO: That pivot gun's got us ranged!

Sound: Impact of another blast, closer.

LANDO: *(CRIES OUT AS THE EXPLOSION KNOCKS HIM BACK-WARD OFF THE RAIL—TOWARD THE SARLAAC)* Whoa, whoa—

LUKE: Lando!

LANDO: *(HIS VOICE TRAILS OFF AS HE GOES OVER THE SIDE, BUT HE HASN'T FALLEN COMPLETELY OFF)* Luke! Han! Pull me back up!

LUKE: Han, Lando's hanging from a line at the starboard rail. When I get your hands free, pull him back up while I take care of that gun.

HAN: Anything. Just get these ropes off.

CHEWBACCA: HOWLS A WARNING.

HAN: *(OVER NEXT)* Chewie says watch for Boba Fett—

Sound: A hiss and belch of rocket motors moves on, as Boba Fett touches down on the deck wearing his backpack flying rig.

FETT: *(VOICE PROCESSED TO DENOTE HIS HELMET)* Drop the lightsaber, farmboy—["—or I'll flashfry you where you stand."]

LUKE: INDICATES ACT OF LIGHTSABER STROKE.

Sound: The lightsaber hums, slices through Fett's carbine with a burst of molten metal, under next.

FETT: GRATES OUT A SOUND OF PAIN AS HE'S KNOCKED SLIGHTLY OFF.

LUKE: And don't call me "farmboy," bounty hunter.

HAN: *(OVER NEXT)* Incoming! Hit the deck!

Sound: Another bolt of energy comes fireballing in from the pivot gun on the sail barge rail. Deck planks explode, etc., under next.

CHEWBACCA: SHRIEKS AS HE'S HIT BY DECK SPLINTERS, PERIPHERAL BLAST, CONCUSSION, ETC.

HAN: Chewie? Where're you hit? Talk to me!

FETT: *(OVER NEXT, FROM SLIGHTLY OFF)* Try my capture cable on for size, Skywalker.

Sound: Fett's cable weapon fires from his forearm, unspooling as it whickers through the air, whistling as it wraps itself around Luke's body and limbs, immobilizing him, under next.

FETT: Even a lightsaber can't cut that alloy.

LUKE: *(INDICATING STRAIN OF GETTING THE SWORD INTO POSITION, VIA SHEER WRIST LEVERAGE, TO SEVER THE CABLE)* Remains to be seen . . .

Sound: The lightsaber makes a banshee wail, severing the metal line with a sharp, spitting burst.

FETT: *(ENDING OVER NEXT)* If you won't be a prisoner, you'll be a corpse! *(REACTS, BEING DOWNED BY PIVOT GUN SHOT)*

Sound: Another pivot gun round comes Dopplering in, under next.

HAN: Hit the deck!

Sound: The round hits close to Fett.

FETT: SHOUTS IN PAIN AND SHOCK, FALLING OFF.

Sound: Clank and clatter of Fett's Mandalorian battle armor, weapons, etc. as he goes sprawling.

HAN: What's goin' on?

LUKE: The cannon blast knocked out Boba Fett, but there's another sand skiff coming our way.

LANDO: *(FROM OFF, INDICATING STRAIN OF CLINGING TO THE LINE)* Han! Chewie! Pull me up!

HAN: Lando!

CHEWBACCA: MUTTERS, "OOOPS, WE FORGOT 'IM!"

LUKE: Haul up that rope, Han. I'll handle the other skiff.

HAN: *(UNDER NEXT)* Wait, don't go!

LUKE: INDICATES DEMANDS OF A LONG LEAP TO THE OTHER SKIFF, OVER NEXT.

Sound: Luke's boots thump the deck as he leaps from his skiff to the other. Lightsaber sounds move off.

HAN: *(TO HIMSELF)* Skywalker, boarding party of one. *(TO CHEWBACCA)* Chewie!

CHEWBACCA: ANSWERS, "RIGHT HERE."

HAN: Don't move or you'll make that wound worse. I found a spear, here . . .

Sound: Han tapping and fumbling with the spear, using it as a cane for the blind, under next.

HAN: Just home me in on Lando's rope.

CHEWBACCA: WOOFS "TO YOUR LEFT. NO, FURTHER," ETC.

LANDO: *(FROM OFF)* Um, Han, you're not still holding that Cloud City thing against me, are you buddy?

HAN: *(TO LANDO, OFF)* Keep your boots on, Lando, I'm comin'! *(TO CHEWBACCA)* Where, Chewie, more to the left?

FETT: MOVES SLIGHTLY ON, PANTING IN PAIN AND HATRED.

CHEWBACCA: BARKS A WARNING TO HAN THAT FETT'S BACK ON HIS FEET.

HAN: What? Boba Fett? *(INDICATES BLINDLY SWINGING THE SPEAR HAFT LIKE A BASEBALL BAT OR A POOL CUE IN A BAR FIGHT)*

Sound: The spear haft cuts the air, under next.

HAN: Where? Back on his feet? Which way, Chewie—?

Sound: The impact of the spear haft whanging Boba Fett's rocket pack, triggering it. Backpack ignition and blare of thrust moving off as Fett goes flailing away out of control, under next.

HAN: Wup! Think I got him.

FETT: HOWLS IN FRUSTRATION AND DISMAY AS HE CORK-SCREWS OFF INTO THE AIR LIKE A RUNAWAY MISSILE, UNDER NEXT.

Sound: Fett clunks headfirst into the hull of the sail barge, off, and goes sliding down it to drop into the Sarlaac pit.

FETT: HIS CRIES DIE AWAY AS HE PLUNGES INTO THE BELLY OF THE BEAST.

HAN: Chewie, sound off! Did I get him?

Sound: The Sarlaac makes a raspy hiss and rattlesnake rattle as it swallows Fett.

HAN: Where's Boba Fett?

CHEWBACCA: TELLS IT BRIEFLY.

HAN: His jetpack went haywire and now he's down the Salaac's throat? But how could—["—that happen even in a battle as crazy as this one?"]

LANDO: *(FROM OFF)* Han, the Sarlaac's sizing me up for dessert!

HAN: Save it, Chewie. *(INDICATES EXERTION OF LYING DOWN AT THE DECK EDGE, ETC., DURING NEXT)* Lando, can you reach the end of the spear?

Sound: The spear haft and butt tap on the skiff's hull as Han tries to bring it within Lando's reach.

LANDO: *(INDICATING JERKS OF HIS HEAD AS HE AVOIDS BEING EYE-GOUGED BY THE SPEAR)* Not if you poke my eye out! You are still sore at me, admit it!

HAN: If I was I'd be using the pointy end. Now grab hold!

LANDO: Lower it!

HAN: I'm trying!

Sound: A volley from the sail barge's deck gun, heavier impact than the pivot gun.

LANDO: Try harder. Luke took out that pivot cannon, but they've got the deck gun firing now.

Sound: Another bolt from the deck gun, this time hitting the skiff.

Crash of exploding hull, groan of the skiff as it heels over sharply on its starboard side.

HAN: *(HOLLERS AS HE ALMOST FALLS)* Whoa, whoa, whoa! Grab my ankles, Chewie! I'm slipping!

CHEWBACCA: HOOTS AND LOWS, HUNKERING OVER TO SEIZE HAN'S ANKLES AND BELAY HIM.

HAN: *(TO CHEWIE)* Good, now hang on!

LANDO: Quit fooling around up there. Something's groping my foot. I think it's the Sarlaac's tentacle.

HAN: Grab the spear! You've almost got it—

Sound: A third heavy round from the deck gun.

HAN: REACTS.

LANDO: REACTS.

HAN: Lando, try again. Gently now. All, all right. Easy, Chewie . . .

LANDO: *(STRUGGLING WITH THE TENTACLE CLUTCHING HIM)* The Sarlaac's got my foot. It's pulling me down!

HAN: *(TO CHEWIE)* Chewie, pass me that gun. *(TO LANDO)* Lando, hang on.

CHEWBACCA: CATERWAULS, PASSING THE BLASTER.

HAN: *(TO CHEWIE)* Hurry, gimme the blaster. *(INDICATES GETTING HIS HAND ON IT)* Got it. *(TO LANDO)* Okay, Lando, don't move!

LANDO: *(INDICATING STRUGGLE TO HANG ON)* No, wait! I thought you were blind!

HAN: It's all right. Trust me.

LANDO: Aim a little higher! No, you're still too low!

HAN: I don't need a consultant, chum. Now hold still . . .

Sound: The blaster fires once, twice.

LANDO: You hit it. *(LAUGHS A BIT HYSTERICALLY)* You got it, it's letting go!

HAN: *(TO CHEWIE)* Haul away, Chewie! Pull us up!

CHEWBACCA: YIPS WITH RELIEF, COMPLYING.

HAN: *(INDICATING HE'S BEING PULLED UP AND TUGGING LANDO IN TURN)* The deck gun's stopped firing. I think Luke got it.

LANDO: *(STRAINING, TOO)* Could we concentrate on me just a little longer?

HAN: If I didn't know better I'd say you were getting soft, Calrissian. Up you come—*(INDICATES LAST YANK TO GET LANDO ON DECK)*

LANDO: *(REACTS)* You look after Chewie. I'll get to the helm.

HAN: What about Boba Fett?

LANDO: He bounced off the side of the barge and went down the Sarlaac's gullet like a jet luge. He's finished.

HAN: But was he dead?

LANDO: The way he hit that hull, his helmet's probably flatter than a Cloud City landing platform. He can't have survived.

HAN: I'm not leaving till I'm sure!

Sound: A distant firing of the deck gun and small arms, some of which mew past POV.

HAN: *(REACTS TO SHOTS)* Then again, I can be flexible. But what about the others?

LANDO: They'll be here. Stand by, bear down, and hang on!

Sound: More cannon fire and small arms racket, yells, off. Scene fades to background as narrator comes up.

NARRATOR: Half a victory can still become a defeat. Leia, Han, Chewie, and the droids have yet to escape the wrath and murderous minions of Jabba the Hutt. Even if they do, this triumph will mark only the opening skirmish of an epic final confrontation with the Empire. Ahead of them waits the planet-obliterating power of a new and even more terrifying Death Star, and beyond that the raw evil of the dark side of the Force. The Rebels are being drawn deep into a web of deception and defeat. At its center waits the most dread entity in the galaxy, a creature no longer truly human: the Emperor Palpatine himself.

Music: Closing theme up under credits.

NARRATOR: CLOSING CREDITS.

EPISODE THREE:

"PROPHESIS AND DESTINIES"

CAST:
Jabba the Hutt
Threepio
Leia
Luke
Han
Lando
Imperial Officer
Moff Jerjerrod
Darth Vader
Yoda
Obi-Wan Kenobi (Ben)
Emperor Palpatine
Sail Guard
Last Guard

SOUND/FX ROLES:
Salacious Crumb
Artoo-Detoo

ANNOUNCER: OPENING CREDITS.

Music: Opening theme.

NARRATOR: A long time ago in a galaxy far, far away there came a time of revolution, when Rebels united to challenge a tyrannical Empire. Now an ultimate confrontation looms near, as the threads of the Emperor Palpatine's master plan draw the Rebel Alliance toward a last, apocalyptic battle.

Sound: Background battle around the Sarlaac pit as per the end of Episode Two, but heard from POV of Jabba's sail barge.

NARRATOR: But above the pit of the monstrous Sarlaac, on the desert planet Tatooine, one small group of freedom fighters is facing its own day of reckoning. There, Luke Skywalker and a band of allies have risked all to free Han Solo from the clutches of the evil gangster Jabba the Hutt.

Sound: More combat, including Luke's lightsaber, Jabba's bellow, chaos among Jabba's hangers-on, etc.

NARRATOR: Han, Lando Calrissian, and Chewbacca are battling guards to liberate a sand skiff. Nearby, on Jabba's great sail barge, all is chaos and carnage. Luke Skywalker is on the attack, lightsaber in hand—to free his other companions, and end Jabba's reign of terror.

SCENE 3-1   INTERIOR JABBA'S SAIL BARGE

Sound: Battle furor up, off.

JABBA: *(SLIGHTLY OFF)* <Oolah loobah cogh!>

Sound: Under preceding. Boba Fett's rocket pack has made a belching approach to near off, ending in a loud bonk signifying the bounty hunter's impact with the ironclad hull by Jabba's banquet cabin.

CROWD: JABBERS, REACTS, IN ASSORTED LINGOES.

LEIA: *(SURREPTITIOUSLY)* Threepio, what was that?

THREEPIO: *(MATCHING HER TONE)* If I understand correctly, Your Highness, Boba Fett just ricocheted off the hull plates and went plummeting down into the Sarlaac.

LEIA: Everybody's busy watching, pass me that statuette.

THREEPIO: Certainly, Your Highness. *(INDICATES EFFORT OF PASSING IT)* But I don't understand why you want it.

LEIA: *(INDICATES TAKING THE HEAVY LITTLE OBJECT)* You will in a second. Stand back.

THREEPIO: But Princess Leia, that instrument panel controls all the power circuits on the barge.

LEIA: Not for long . . .

SALACIOUS CRUMB: GIVES ONE OF HIS MANIACAL LAUGHS, OFF, THEN GIBBERS ACCUSATIONS AT THEM.

THREEPIO: Salacious Crumb—get away, you heinous little imp! *(TO LEIA)* What a torment he's made of my life!

LEIA: Threepio, go find Artoo. I need him to get this chain off me.

Sound: Leia rattles her chain.

THREEPIO: But what about Jabba?

LEIA: I'll deal with him. *(INDICATING EFFORT OF SWINGING THE STATUETTE, OVER NEXT)* Now . . . stand . . . back . . .

Sound: The improvised hammer smashes the fragile control box.

Energy spatters, circuits short, chips fry, and solder explodes. Crystal components shatter and deep, ominous vibes come from the power-routing systemry.

CROWD: DIVERSE BLEATS OF CONSTERNATION.

JABBA: *(OFF)* <Mootah teekay kalpa miti!>

THREEPIO: Your Highness, you'll blow the barge apart! With us aboard!

LEIA: Go get Artoo! Fast!

THREEPIO: *(MOVING OFF)* Good grief, the end is upon us!

JABBA: <Aarrghh! Poosak tawa ch'upa, Leia!>

LEIA: That's right, Jabba: You forgot one thing.

Sound: She gathers the slack of the heavy chain, to use it as a weapon of revenge.

LEIA: *(INDICATING EFFORT OF ATTACKING HIM, TO GARROTE HIM WITH THE HEAVY CHAIN)* When you put a slave on a leash . . . the other end is attached to you!

JABBA: TRUMPETS IN DISMAY AND OUTRAGE AS SHE LEAPS BEHIND HIM, THROWING THE LOOP OF CHAIN AROUND HIS (WELL, KIND OF NONEXISTENT) NECK AND TIGHTENING IT.

LEIA: *(THROUGH GRITTED TEETH, AS SHE SLOWLY CHOKES THE LIFE OUT OF HIM)* Now you know how it feels to have cold iron around your throat, Jabba!

JABBA: GASPS AND GURGLES, TRIES SUMMONING ASSISTANCE.

LEIA: Call for help all you want. *(GRUNTS WITH EFFORT; SHE'S GOT HER KNEE IN HIS BACK, HAULING BACK HARD ON THE CHAIN GARROTE)* Your fine pack of cutthroats are too busy saving their own necks.

JABBA: WHEEZING AND STRANGLING.

CRUMB: GIBBERS FROM NEAR OFF, HISSING MENACINGLY. MAKES ANGRY GHOULIE NOISES, AND A YELL AS HE HURLS THINGS AT HER, OVER NEXT.

Sound: Sound of metal platter bouncing from the throne, crystal goblet shattering, etc.

LEIA: Get away, you little gargoyle! *(INDICATES DODGING AND SHRUGGING OFF THE BOMBARDMENT)*

CRUMB: LAUGHS MANIACALLY.

THREEPIO: *(MOVING ON)* Artoo is coming, Your Highness! We must—["must abandon the sail barge before it's too late."] Oh, Salacious Crumb!

CRUMB: TAUNTS AND PRATTLES AS HE ATTACKS THREEPIO, OVER NEXT.

THREEPIO: I'll save you, Princess Leia!

Sound: Robotic servos and clattering, sounds of struggle, under next.

THREEPIO: *(INDICATING THE FIGHT)* Leave her alone, you mis-begotten gnome!

Sound: Explosion from abovedecks and elsewhere, as more power-routing malfunctions pound the sail barge.

THREEPIO: REACTS.

CRUMB: REACTS.

Sound: Knocked off balance, Threepio and Crumb go rattling and clashing to the deck.

CRUMB: *(MOVING OFF WITH THREEPIO)* CACKLES AND FROTHS.

LEIA: *(INDICATES SHE'S EXERTING ALL HER STRENGTH AND*

LEVERAGE TO FINISH HIM OFF) Here's your . . . final payment . . . Jabba . . .

JABBA: MASSIVE DEATH RATTLES.

Sound: Impact of his giant tail, beating the deck like a slowing funeral drum.

JABBA: EXPIRES MESSILY, FINISHING UNDER NEXT.

Sound: Deck-shaking thud as Jabba collapses dead.

LEIA: *(OUT OF BREATH FROM THE EPIC CONTEST)* You're out of business.

Sound: Artoo running noises as the astromech moves on.

ARTOO: *(MOVING ON)* FLUTES AND PIPES AN URGENT HAIL.

THREEPIO: Artoo! Hurry, cut the princess's chain . . . with your laser torch. *(TO CRUMB)* As for you, you abomination—perhaps a box on the ear will change your ways. *(INDICATES EFFORT OF THUMPING CRUMB A GOOD ONE)*

Sound: Thump as Threepio drubs him one.

CRUMB: SCEECHES IN PAIN.

ARTOO: MOVES ON WITH A BURST OF SOUND, OVER NEXT.

Sound: Artoo comes to a halt. There's the snap of a latch opening in Artoo's upper body, the laser welding/cutting tool extending from the droid's interior. Laser hums and fires as a chain link hisses and parts.

LEIA: Good! *(UNDER NEXT)* That's got it.

Sound: Chain rattles as she parts it, drops the long end.

LEIA: Come on, we've got to get above decks.

ARTOO: PIPES "LEAD THE WAY."

Sound: Under preceding, sounds of the struggle between Threepio and Salacious Crumb, who's gotten the upper hand as they struggle on the deck.

CRUMB: TITTERS SADISTICALLY AND BLATHERS AS HE TEARS AT THREEPIO'S PHOTORECEPTOR.

THREEPIO: *(OVER PRECEDING)* No, not my eye! Artoo! Get this odious little fiend off me!

LEIA: Help him, Artoo. *(MOVING OFF)* I'll meet you on deck.

ARTOO: TWEEDLES A RESPONSE.

Sound: Artoo opens another small port in his side, deploys his electro-tines, fires a crackling bolt of energy with a voltage hum to it. The blistering and singeing of Crumb's scorched rump are heard, under next.

CRUMB: SHRILLS IN PAIN AND SURPRISE.

THREEPIO: Well struck, Artoo!

CRUMB: WAILS IN PAIN, SCAMPERING OFF.

THREEPIO: My poor eye! Artoo, what's to become of us?

ARTOO: ANSWERS HASTILY, MOVING OFF.

THREEPIO: "Exit strategy?" What exit strategy? *(MOVING OFF)* Why has no one told me anything about a rescue plan?

SCENE 3-2 OPEN DECK OF JABBA'S SAIL BARGE

Sound: Belowdecks fades. Open main deck of the sail barge comes up. More explosions shake the ship's vitals in background. Random shots wheep back and forth. Luke's lightsaber hums, flaring and crashing when it repels gun beams, under next.

LUKE: Leia! Over here!

LEIA: *(MOVING ON)* Luke—watch out behind you!

LUKE: INDICATES ACT OF WHIRLING, STRIKING WITH THE SWORD.

Sound: Lightsaber blares, dealing a lethal stroke.

SAIL GUARD: YOWLS IN DEATH AGONY, FALLING BACK OFF.

LEIA: Where're the others?

LUKE: Waiting in the skiff, but we've got to finish off this barge. Take the deck gun controls and point the barrel at the deck.

LEIA: *(MOVING SLIGHTLY OFF)* I'm on it.

Sound: Leia clambers onto the gun mount, works controls. Heavy servos, etc., as the deck gun traverses and depresses to train on the deck itself.

LUKE: Where're the droids?

Sound: Artoo's and Threepio's noises of locomotion moving on, under next.

THREEPIO: *(MOVING ON)* Here we are, Master Luke!

ARTOO: TRILLS A GREETING.

LUKE: Good. Get ready, Artoo.

ARTOO: ACKNOWLEDGES, GIVES THREEPIO MARCHING ORDERS.

THREEPIO: "Move to the rail?" *(INDICATES BEING BULLDOZED ALONG BY ARTOO.)* Very well, Artoo, only stop butting into me!

LUKE: It'll be all right, Threepio. Now hurry.

THREEPIO: Artoo, where are we going? *(MOVING OFF)* I couldn't possibly jump to the ground from here.

LEIA: Relax, Threepio. It's all part of the exit strategy.

ARTOO: ELABORATES A BIT ON THAT.

THREEPIO: Lando will get us with a hoist? But, I don't want to be hoisted—ah!

Sound: Artoo rams Threepio over the side with a hollow thud.

THREEPIO: *(TRAILING AWAY OFF AS HE PLUNGES)* Artoo, no-oooo!

ARTOO: BEEPS "GERONIMO," AND CASTS HIMSELF OVERBOARD AS WELL, HIS SIGNALS FADING AWAY.

LEIA: The deck gun's ready, Luke.

LUKE: Just let me grab this rope. We'll swing across to the skiff. *(INDICATES GRABBING THE LINE OF RIGGING, MOVING TO HER SIDE)* Okay, grab me and hang on tight. When I kick the switch we go. Once that cannon fires, this barge is a goner.

LEIA: Feels kind of familiar, doesn't it?

LUKE: Practice makes perfect. Ready?

Sound: Luke kicks the foot-pedal deck gun trigger. Deck gun fires into the barge's deck in a terrific blast, setting off secondary explosions belowdecks, etc.

LUKE: Hold tight! *(LETS OUT A TRIUMPHANT WHOOP AS HE SWINGS OFF, VOICE FADING)*

LEIA: *(JOINS IN, CROWING A VICTORY CRY, MOVING OFF)*

Sound: More explosions well up, Jabba's sail barge in its death throes. Maybe a terrified final scream from that malefic little bogey, Salacious Crumb. A climactic explosion blots out all other sound, then fades, along with the scene.

SCENE 3-3 *MILLENNIUM FALCON* COCKPIT

Sound: Ship's "getaway" noises, engines revving high as she accelerates, etc.

HAN: X-wing, this is the *Millennium Falcon*.

Sound: He flicks various switches on the console.

HAN: Luke, where are you? Can Artoo get a navicomputer reading?

LUKE: *(OVER COCKPIT COMMO)* No need, we're right behind you.

LANDO: Stick close, Luke. We're not out of the woods yet.

HAN: We never will be, flying at this altitude. We're liable to knock some Tusken Raider off his bantha.

Sound: Warning indicator alarm starts toning, under next.

LEIA: We can't go for altitude yet. Check your long-range sensors and you'll see why.

HAN: Whoo! Imperial battle group. Star Destroyers, the works.

LEIA: Just waiting to jump any Rebel assault force that tried to rescue you from Jabba's.

LANDO: Which is why we had to go with Luke's plan.

Sound: Threepio approaching.

71

THREEPIO: *(MOVING ON)* Sir—first mate Chewbacca's wounds are stabilized and he is resting comfortably.

LANDO: He's a tough old cuss. He'll be up and around in no time.

HAN: *(TO COMMO)* Luke, that blockade's holding the high ground. We'd have a better chance of tunneling our way off of Tatooine.

LUKE: *(OVER COMMO)* Take a look back at Jabba's, Han.

Sound: More instrumentation, as sensors image the situation back at the Hutt's palace.

HAN: I still can't see too well. Looks like a flotilla lifting off.

LUKE: *(OVER COMMO)* Smuggler ships, corsair gunboats, slave transports—everything that can get into the air. Y'know why?

HAN: Tell me.

LANDO: You can thank Artoo-Detoo.

HAN: Artoo?

ARTOO: TWEEDLES MODESTLY, OVER COMMO—BEING IN THE TECH SOCKET OF LUKE'S X-WING.

LANDO: Artoo penetrated Jabba's data system. His toadies think the Imperials are coming for them with death warrants. So they're gonna try to blast their way offworld.

LEIA: And in the meantime we slip out the back door.

HAN: A little "Corellian Overdrive," huh?

LANDO: Looks like the fireworks are starting, up there. What a free-for-all.

LUKE: You ready to run for it, Han?

HAN: Full-bore, Luke.

Sound: Han and Lando flipping switches. Falcon sounds build.

LUKE: Pour it on, and don't stop for anything.

Sound: Brief transition, as Falcon *and* X-wing *make escape, leaving Tatooine behind.*

LEIA: That's it, we're out of Tatooine's atmosphere.

HAN: Talk to me, Threepio. What do the lookdown sensors see?

THREEPIO: Imagery shows intense fighting at various altitudes, but we are clear of all pursuit.

HAN: Gotta hand it to you, Luke: right past an Imperial blockade without firing a shot.

LUKE: *(OVER COMMO)* The Force was with us, Han. I'll see you all back at the fleet rendezvous.

LANDO: Clear skies, Luke.

LEIA: And don't be late. The Alliance will be assembling by now.

LUKE: I won't.

THREEPIO: Artoo, do try to restrain that impetuous nature of yours!

ARTOO: MOOGS A GOOD-BYE.

HAN: Hey, Luke . . .

LUKE: *(OVER COMMO)* Yeah, Han?

HAN: Thanks for comin' after me. Now I owe you one.

SCENE 3-4 X-WING COCKPIT

Sound: Brief transtion to Luke's cockpit. Luke flipping switches, etc.

LUKE: Artoo, prepare to lay a course in the navicomputer.

ARTOO: TRILLS A QUESTION.

LUKE: What, my hand? No, it's fine. A blaster shot just grazed it.

ARTOO: PRESSES THE ISSUE.

LUKE: No, it doesn't hurt. I don't let it. *(SHAKING OFF THE MOOD)* Okay, course plotted. Get ready to jump into hyperspace.

ARTOO: WHISTLES A QUERY.

LUKE: That's right, we're going to the Dagobah system. I have a promise to keep . . . to an old friend.

SCENE 3-5A *MILLENNIUM FALCON* COCKPIT

Sound: Characteristic Falcon *environment.*

HAN: Threepio, what's holding up that hyperdrive diagnostic?

THREEPIO: Sorry, sir. My damaged photoreceptor appears to be giving me a bit of double vision.

LEIA: Threepio, are you all right?

THREEPIO: Well . . .

LEIA: I'm sorry we couldn't let you in on Luke's rescue plan, Threepio.

THREEPIO: No. I quite understand the logic of it, Your Highness. My memory banks are more open to scrutiny than Artoo's.

LANDO: When Ninedenine scanned you and found no sign of subterfuge, it put Jabba off his guard.

HAN: Corellian Overdrive, Threepio.

THREEPIO: I'm not sure I fully comprehend that turn of phrase, sir.

HAN: Corellian Overdrive is doing whatever you need to do to get where you need to go, Threepio. Including finagling the rules—

LEIA: "Lying."

HAN:—rejiggering the operational parameters—

LANDO: "Stacking the deck."

HAN: Hey, Corellian Overdrive doesn't mean cheating in an honest game.

LANDO: I seem to recall some angry cardplayers who saw it differently, Han.

THREEPIO: Put that way, perhaps Corellian Overdrive was called for.

LEIA: And, Threepio, thank you for defending me from Salacious Crumb. It was very brave of you.

Sound: Lando's chair squeaking as he rises, under next.

LANDO: *(INDICATES EFFORT OF RISING FROM HIS CHAIR, AS HE ADDRESSES THREEPIO)* C'mon back to the tech station, Threepio. We'll see if we can't get your eye back in focus.

THREEPIO: *(MOVING OFF WITH LANDO)* That would be most appreciated, sir, thank you. And thank you, Your Highness.

SCENE 3-5B *MILLENNIUM FALCON* **COCKPIT**

Sound: Ship noises and a few more toggles thrown, in the silence between Han and Leia.

LEIA: You're welcome, Han.

HAN: Huh?

LEIA: Just making it easy for you. You are sitting there trying to figure out a way to thank me, aren't you?

HAN: I was getting to it, I was getting to it.

LEIA: And?

HAN: Mmm . . . not a bad rescue, for a princess.

LEIA: Compared to yours, you mean? How well planned the Death Star foray was, for instance?

HAN: You're not in that detention cell anymore, are you?

LEIA: You're not in that carbonite slab anymore, are you?

HAN: Awright, awright . . .

LEIA: And while you're replying in kind, what about the last thing I said to you in Cloud City? Just before Vader froze you?

HAN: Whew, a lot of that's kinda blurry, Leia—

LEIA: Never mind. It'll come back to you.

Sound: The console tones with a navigation program-ready signal.

HAN: Um, looks like we're about ready for the jump to hyperspace.

LEIA: Well, I'm sure you can handle that. So if you'll excuse me, Captain—*(INDICATING EFFORT OF RISING, PREPARING TO LEAVE THE COCKPIT)*—I'll go find some clothes that don't require a cabaret permit.

HAN: Huh? Hey, Leia . . .

LEIA: Well?

HAN: You, uh, gonna throw those ones away?

LEIA: *(MOVING OFF)* We'll see. *(REACTING TO ENCOUNTERING LANDO IN THE COCKPIT HATCHWAY)* Whoops. Sorry, Lando.

LANDO: *(REACTS TO BUMPING INTO HER, CHUCKLES)* A distinct pleasure, Princess. Where ya going?

LEIA: Mm-hmm *(MOVING COMPLETELY OFF)* I'll go throw on something a little more . . . durable.

LANDO: *(TO LEIA)* Understandable, but a pure crime against art, Your Highness.

HAN: I thought you were repairing Threepio.

LANDO: Chewie's handling it. So, what d'you think of your baby, Han? Supple and bewitching, isn't she?

HAN: Don't push your luck, Lando.

LANDO: Hey, what's got up your afterburner? I'm talking about the *Falcon*.

HAN: Oh. That.

LANDO: *(MOVING COMPLETELY ON, INDICATING THAT HE'S SIT-TING INTO CO-PILOT'S CHAIR, DURING NEXT)* I put a lot of sweat and money into her while you were in cold storage.

Sound: Co-pilot chair squeaks, etc., as Lando sits.

HAN: Yeah, well, the way I heard it you almost wrecked her on Coruscant.

LANDO: Relax, pal.

HAN: Gimme a break, Lando, letting Threepio fly the *Falcon*?

LANDO: We made it, didn't we?

HAN: Okay. Let's drop it. Navicomputer's got the course laid in for this jump to nowhere.

LANDO: Not nowhere, Han. Every ship the Alliance can scrape together is gonna be there.

HAN: For what?

LANDO: This little scrap coming up is going to be for the whole pot, winner take all.

HAN: What!?

LANDO: The Empire's working on a second Death Star. If they complete it, that'll be the end for the Rebellion.

HAN: *(INDICATING THAT HE'S SNAPPING SWITCHES, PUNCHING BUTTONS)* And I was hoping for a little rest.

LANDO: Afraid not. History won't wait.

Sound: The starship's hyperspace drive sounds build to a crescendo, under next.

HAN: If there's no way around it and no way back . . . we might as well get moving and meet it head-on . . . Hang on!

Sound: Millennium Falcon's *hyperspace drive revs high, ending in that characteristic boom as the ship goes superluminal.*

SCENE 3-6 DEATH STAR SHUTTLE HANGAR BAY

Sound: TIE fighters are heard howling past, flying patrol around Death Star. Shuttle hangar bay comes up, wild lines indicating flight landing operations, machinery, automatons. Warning tones alerting personnel to the arrival of Vader's shuttle.

IMPERIAL OFFICER: *(TO OFF)* Lord Vader's shuttle has entered the hangar bay field.

Sound: Troops' footsteps as they scurry to form ranks.

JERJERROD: *(MOVING ON)* Colonel, what is the meaning of this?

IMPERIAL OFFICER: *(ANNOUNCING TO ALL PRESENT)* Battle station commander on deck!

JERJERROD: Why wasn't I informed that Lord Vader was coming?

IMPERIAL OFFICER: We received no advance word, Moff Jerjerrod. Lord Vader's shuttle simply arrived and—["—demanded landing clearance."]

JERJERROD: Never mind that now. Have your men stand ready.

Sound: Stormtroopers going to present arms, heels clicking, rifles slapped by troopers' gauntleted hands, etc.

SCENE 3-7   SHUTTLE BAY

Sound: Vader's breathing approaches, under next.

JERJERROD: Greetings, Lord Vader. This is an, er, unexpected pleasure.

VADER: *(MOVING ON)* You may dispense with the pleasantries, Moff Jerjerrod. I'm here to put completion of the Death Star back on schedule.

JERJERROD: My lord, my men are working as fast as they can.

VADER: And still this battle station hangs here in the sky over

Endor like a gutted moon. Perhaps I can find new ways to motivate your people.

JERJERROD: I tell you, the Death Star will be operational as planned.

VADER: The Emperor does not share your optimistic appraisal of the situation.

JERJERROD: But he asks the impossible. I need more men.

VADER: Perhaps you can tell him that yourself when he arrives.

JERJERROD: The, the Emperor is coming here?

VADER: Indeed, and he is most displeased with your apparent lack of progress.

JERJERROD: We shall redouble our efforts, my lord!

VADER: I hope so for your sake, Moff Jerjerrod. Our Emperor is not as forgiving as I am.

SCENE 3-8   DAGOBAH SWAMP, INTERIOR YODA'S HUT

Sound: Outside, mournful hoots and hungry hunting cries of teeming wildlife. Thunder and lightning. Rootleaf stew bubbling over the fire, crackle of the flames, etc. Rain on the hut roof. Yoda's cane tap-taps slowly on the floor as he moves with a pained, aged slowness.

YODA: Hmm. That face you make, Luke Skywalker. Look I so old to your young eyes?

LUKE: *(GUILTILY)* No, Master Yoda—of course not.

YODA: *(CHUCKLES RUEFULLY)* I do, yes! Sick have I become. Old and weak. When nine hundred years old you reach, look as good you will not, hmm?

LUKE: Master, forgive me but—you mustn't talk like that.

YODA: Soon I will rest. Yes, forever sleep. Earned it, I have. But for now . . . *(INDICATING EFFORT OF CLIMBING UP ONTO HIS SLEEPING SHELF PALLET)* . . . lie down, I must, for weary am I.

LUKE: Master Yoda, you can't die.

YODA: Speak not so! Strong am I with the Force, but not so strong as to defy death. Nor would I choose to be. Twilight is upon me and soon night must fall. That is the way of all things . . . the way of the Force.

LUKE: But I need your help. I've come back to complete my training. This time I won't stop until you're satisfied. Until you've taught me everything I need to know about the Force and about being a Jedi Knight.

YODA: No more training do you require. *(SIGHS, ARRANGING HIMSELF ON HIS BED, OVER NEXT)*

Sound: Yoda shifts, preparing to sleep.

YODA: Already know you that which you need.

LUKE: Then I am a Jedi.

YODA: Ohh, not yet. One thing remains: Vader. You must confront Vader. Then—only then—a Jedi you will be. And confront him you will.

LUKE: Master Yoda . . . is Darth Vader my father?

YODA: Mmm . . . rest I need. Yes . . . rest.

LUKE: Yoda, I must know. I look to you for the truth, Master.

YODA: Your father he is—the Dark Lord of the Sith. Told you this, did he?

LUKE: Yes. In Cloud City, on Bespin.

YODA: Unexpected this is, and unfortunate . . .

LUKE: Unfortunate that I know the truth at last?

YODA: No, Luke. Unfortunate that you rushed to face him. That incomplete was your training when you confronted his power. That not ready were you for the burden of this truth, and the weight of this struggle.

LUKE: I'm sorry I let you down. I did what I thought I had to. I don't see how letting my friends be killed could be right.

YODA: Whatever the future brings now, remember: A Jedi's strength flows from the Force. But beware. Anger, fear, aggression. The dark side are they. Once you start down the dark path, forever will it dominate your destiny. Luke . . . Luke . . .

Sound: Some effect that suggests Yoda's derezzing, under next.

LUKE: Master Yoda, you're slipping away. I can feel it, I can see it.

YODA: Do not . . . do not underestimate the powers of the Emperor, or suffer your father's fate you will. Luke, when gone am I . . . the last of the Jedi will you be.

LUKE: You can't go.

YODA: Luke, the Force runs strong in your family. Pass on what you have learned.

LUKE: Master, you can't cross over yet. Please!

YODA: Hear me you must. Luke . . . there is . . . another Sky . . . Skywalker . . . *(SIGHS AND EXPIRES)*

Sound: Yoda's derezzing S/FX fade.

LUKE: Master? Come back. Without your help I'll fail. *(TO HIMSELF MORE THAN YODA, WHO'S GONE)* Don't go. Don't go.

SCENE 3-9   DAGOBAH EXTERIOR, NEAR LUKE'S X-WING

Sound: External Dagobah comes up. Artoo's running noises in near background, various servos and efectuators as the droid helps prep the X-wing for departure.

ARTOO: TOOTLES AN INTERROGATIVE TO LUKE.

LUKE: What, Artoo? No, leave all of Yoda's things here. They belong here.

ARTOO: A SAD LITTLE CONSOLING NOISE.

LUKE: I can't do it, Artoo. I can't go on alone.

BEN: *(OFF, VOICE PROCESSED TO INDICATE GHOSTLY VISITATION)* Yoda will always be with you, Luke.

LUKE: Ben!?

BEN: You must bear in mind what Yoda taught you, Luke. Your destiny comes swiftly upon you now.

LUKE: Why didn't you tell me the truth? You told me Vader betrayed and murdered my father.

BEN: Your father was seduced by the dark side of the Force. He ceased to be Anakin Skywalker and became Darth Vader. When that happened, the good man who was your father was destroyed. So what I told you was true . . . from a certain point of view.

LUKE: A certain point of view?

BEN: Your father was betrayed and murdered . . . by the man he himself became. Luke, you're going to find that many of the truths we cling to depend greatly on our own point of view.

LUKE: You let me think I was training to face my father's killer, not to slay my own flesh and blood.

BEN: When I first knew him, your father was already a great pilot.

But I was amazed how strongly the Force was with him. I took it upon myself to train him as a Jedi. I thought that I could instruct him just as well as Yoda might have. I was wrong.

LUKE: There is still good in him, Ben.

BEN: He's more machine now than man. Twisted and evil.

LUKE: I can't do what you expect of me.

BEN: You must face Darth Vader again. You cannot escape your destiny, Luke.

LUKE: I can't kill my own father.

BEN: Then the Emperor has already won. You were our new hope, our only hope.

LUKE: But—Yoda spoke of another.

BEN: The other he spoke of is your twin sister.

LUKE: I have no sister.

BEN: To protect you both from the Emperor you were hidden from your father when you were born. The Emperor knew, as I did, that if Anakin were to have any offspring they would be a threat even to Palpatine's vast power. That is the reason why your sister has remained safely anonymous.

LUKE: And yet sometimes I sense that "other" out there, her blood the same as mine. Someone I've never quite seen through the mist but someone I've always known. Someone I know so well . . . *(SOTTO VOCE)* Leia! Leia's my sister.

BEN: Your insight serves you well. But bury your feelings deep down, Luke. They do you credit but they could be made to serve the Emperor.

LUKE: Yoda felt Leia was another hope for defeating the Emperor.

BEN: So he said, but your sister has had no training as a Jedi.

LUKE: Maybe it doesn't have anything to do with being a Jedi. Maybe Leia has some destiny beyond the Jedi way.

BEN: You mustn't deceive yourself, Luke, and you mustn't conjure up false hope. Vader's vision isn't clouded by sentiment, nor is the Emperor's. And if yours is, when you face them at last, you will be destroyed.

SCENE 3-10   DEATH STAR SHUTTLE BAY

Sound: Sounds of the Emperor's shuttle setting down, bay deckplates resounding, etc., under next.

VADER: Your troops are ready, Moff Jerjerrod? The Emperor will be debarking from his shuttle as soon as it touches down, without further ceremony.

Sound: Noises, off, of the shuttle ramp being lowered and the airlock hatch opening with a depressurizing hiss, under next.

JERJERROD: Yes, Lord Vader.

Sound: The slow tread of the Emperor moves on, accompanied by the tapping of his cane—a different aural quality and cadence from Yoda's—under next.

VADER: Greetings, my Emperor. I kneel before you and wait to execute your will.

EMPEROR: *(MOVING ON)* Rise, my faithful friend. Come, walk at my side.

Sound: Vader's bootsteps, Emperor's tapping, signify a cursory, nonchalant inspection of troops and battle station.

EMPEROR: You have hastened construction most effectively—and at such a paltry cost in lives.

VADER: The Death Star will be completed on schedule.

EMPEROR: You have done well, Lord Vader. And now I sense you wish to continue your search for young Skywalker.

VADER: Yes, my master.

EMPEROR: Patience, my friend. In time he will seek you out. And when he does, you must bring him before me. He has grown strong in the Force. Only together can we turn him to the dark side.

VADER: As you wish, so shall it be.

EMPEROR: Everything is proceeding as I have forseen. *(CHUCK-LES, SAVORING THE COMING VICTORY)* Come, we will repair to my throne room and give thought to other preparations.

SCENE 3-11   EMPEROR'S THRONE ROOM

Sound: A quieter chamber but with echoes to indicate size, absence of onlookers. Some instrumentation but it's not a technical facility.

JERJERROD: Your seat of power pleases you, my Emperor?

EMPEROR: It suffices, Moff Jerjerrod. Now hear your overlord's command.

VADER: What is thy bidding, my master?

EMPEROR: Send our sector starfleet to the far side of Endor. There it will stay until called for.

VADER: But what of the reports of the Rebel fleet massing near Sullust?

EMPEROR: The Alliance's ragtag armada is of no concern. Soon the Rebellion will be crushed and young Skywalker will be one of us! Your work here is finished, my friend. Go to the command ship and await my orders.

VADER: Yes, my master.

EMPEROR: And await, as well, the coming of the Alliance here, into our very grip. Await the final crushing of those who oppose us. Await, in good discipline, the coming of Luke Skywalker, and a magnificent new day for the dark side of the Force.

Sound: Throne room fades.

NARRATOR: Like the energies of some huge weather system converging in an apocalyptic storm, events swirl all players in the galactic drama toward the peaceful green moon of the planet Endor and the vast war machine poised above it. Starships mass for battle, and the mightiest weapon system in the known universe is readied to meet them. Combatants of all species brace themselves as best they can for what is now to come. With a leap across the dark light-years, the two sides will grapple at last to a final outcome. And in the heart of a young warrior named Luke Skywalker, who is fated to be either the first of the new Jedi or the last of the old, the two sides of light and darkness will lock in a mortal duel as well . . . with the fate of a galaxy riding on the outcome.

Music: Closing theme, under credits.

NARRATOR: CLOSING CREDITS.

EPISODE FOUR:

"PATTERN AND WEB"

CAST:
Luke
General Madine
Lando
Han
Leia
Threepio
Mon Mothma
Admiral Ackbar
Rebel Controller
Imperial Scout #1
Death Star Controller
Imperial Scout #2
Scout #3
Scout #4

SOUND/FX ROLES:
Chewbacca
Artoo-Detoo
Wicket

ANNOUNCER: OPENING CREDITS.

Music: Opening theme.

NARRATOR: A long time ago in a galaxy far, far away there came a time of revolution, when Rebels united to challenge a tyrannical Empire. Now the final act of this cosmic struggle races toward its climax. The Empire's new and more powerful Death Star nears completion, preparing to unleash planet-crushing power and give its overlords ironclad dominion over the galaxy.

Sound: Snub fighters zazzing past, and the heavier thunder of the Rebel frigate and other starships of the line.

NARRATOR: But around the planet Sullust, the total resources of the Rebel Alliance have been marshaled for one ultimate, desperate attempt to smash the Imperial juggernaut. Every spaceworthy snub fighter, every fighting ship and combat unit has been assembled in a makeshift armada. From Sullust there can be no going back. After Sullust there can only come freedom or oblivion. Aboard the Headquarters Frigate, flagship of the Alliance Fleet, the Rebels await their briefing for the great assault, among them a group of friends just back from Tatooine. And if there has been little time for rest and recuperation, still the layover at Sullust has brought about some definite changes.

SCENE 4–1 MAIN REBEL BRIEFING ROOM

Sound: Ambient noises of the Rebel main briefing room (war room) come up with sounds of systemry and instrumentation, murmuring voices human and non-, tracking displays and holographics fields, etc.

GENERAL MADINE: *(OFF)* If you'll all find your seats, please. Chief Counsellor Mon Mothma and Admiral Ackbar will be here momentarily to conduct the primary briefing. *(TO LANDO)* Would all Assault Wing pilots report to General Calrissian.

HAN: *(MOVING ON)* Hey there—General?

LANDO: Han!

HAN: 'Scuse me, I wanted to tell you: If you ever need a double to trick the Imperials, I know this guy named Lando who looks exactly like you.

LANDO: What are you babbling about?

HAN: This fella Lando's not a general, see. He's a lady's man and a card cheat with a terrible reputation.

LANDO: "Cheat?" Every time you pick up an honest deck the face cards start crying.

HAN: Why, Lando, it is you! *(TO OFF)* Hey, Leia! Chewie! C'mere and take a look at the man who's gonna pop the Death Star like a balloon!

CHEWBACCA: WOOFS IN GREETING AND AMUSEMENT, MOVING ON.

LEIA: *(MOVING ON)* Congratulations, Lando. Don't pay any attention to Han. He's just jealous. When he went into the carbonite he was the best-looking pilot in the Rebellion.

THREEPIO: *(MOVING ON)* General Calrissian, you cut an extremely dashing figure in that uniform, if I may say so.

LANDO: Thanks, Threepio.

HAN: So they made you an Assault Wing commander, huh Lando?

LANDO: Somebody must've told the general's staff about my little maneuver at the Battle of Taanab.

HAN: Well don't look at me, pal. I just said you were a fair pilot. I didn't know they were lookin' for somebody to lead this crazy attack.

MADINE: *(OFF)* Seats, please. Seats. Mon Mothma, leader of our Alliance, will begin the briefing as soon as we're ready.

Sound: Chairs slide, benches squeak and scrape, as the assembled fighters from many species find seats.

LANDO: Leia, any word from Luke?

LEIA: No. But he won't let us down.

THREEPIO: The last communication from Artoo indicated his presence in the Dagobah system.

HAN: Slide over, Chewie. You're taking up three places.

CHEWBACCA: WUFFS, SHIFTING.

LANDO: I'm surprised they didn't ask you to fly lead for the assault, Han.

HAN: *(INDICATES TAKING A SEAT AS WELL)* Who says they didn't? But I ain't crazy. You're the respectable one, remember?

LEIA: Shh. Do you mind if we finish the Rebellion before you two sort out bragging rights?

MON MOTHMA: *(SLIGHTLY OFF, ADDRESSING ASSEMBLY)* Greetings to you all, my comrades-in-arms. Time is short, and so I'll direct your attention to the holographic display of the new Death Star.

LANDO: It's only half built. Looks like a rotted-out metal tooth.

LEIA: For once, we're a jump ahead of the Emperor.

MON MOTHMA: The Emperor has made a critical error, and the

time for our attack has come. The data brought to us by the Bothan spies pinpoints the exact location of the new battle station. We also know that the weapons systems of this Death Star are not yet operational. With the Imperial fleet spread throughout the galaxy, the station is relatively unprotected.

HAN: *(ASIDE, SOFTLY)* "Relative" is right, when you're talking about starfleet battle wagons.

LEIA: Shh.

MON MOTHMA: But most important of all, we've learned that the Emperor himself is personally overseeing the final stages of the construction of the Death Star. Many Bothans died to bring us this information. *(TO ACKBAR)* Admiral Ackbar, if you will present the strategic overview, please.

Sound: Incidental noises of the holographic display, computer-driven modeling, under next.

ACKBAR: *(OFF)* As this modeling shows, the battle station's orbiting the forest moon of the planet Endor. Although the weapons systems are not yet operational, this Death Star does have a strong defense mechanism. It is protected by an energy shield that is generated from a large installation on the nearby forest moon.

HAN: *(ASIDE)* "Strong?" Like a bonded-armor wall two parsecs thick.

THREEPIO: It does seem impenetrable, sir.

ACKBAR: The defensive shield must be disabled by a ground commando operation before any attack on the Death Star can be attempted. Once the energy shield is down, our cruisers will establish a perimeter, holding any opposition at bay while our fighters fly into the Death Star's superstructure and knock out its main reactor. General Calrissian has volunteered to lead the fighter attack.

CROWD: SCATTERING OF APPLAUSE, WILD LINES—MURMURS OF APPROVAL BUT ALSO OF MISGIVING.

HAN: Good luck, General. You're gonna need it.

LANDO: It hasn't let me down so far, Han.

ACKBAR: General Madine, if you'll recap the commando operation.

MADINE: Thank you, Admiral Ackbar. *(TO ASSEMBLY)* We have stolen a small Imperial shuttle, the *Tydirium*, disguised it as a re-supply ship, and using a secret Imperial code, a strike team will land on the forest moon and destroy the installation there with demolitions, deactivating the shield generator and leaving the Death Star without its protective shield.

LANDO: *(ASIDE)* I wonder who they found to go strolling into that nest of stormtroopers?

HAN: Probably some sucker who lost a coin flip.

THREEPIO: The assignment sounds suicidally dangerous.

MADINE: *(TO HAN)* General Solo, is your strike team assembled?

LEIA: Han?

HAN: *(TO MADINE)* Um, yessir, my combat team's ready.

LEIA: Who'd you lose the coin flip to, Han? Yourself?

HAN: You could say that. 'N' now look at me. A volunteer. *(TO MADINE)* General, I don't have a command crew for the shuttle yet.

CHEWBACCA: INSISTS THAT HE'S GOING.

HAN: *(TO CHEWBACCA)* Well, it's gonna be rough, pal. I didn't want to speak for you.

CHEWBACCA: REITERATES.

HAN: *(TO MADINE)* Okay, that's one, sir.

LEIA: *(TO MADINE)* Um, General Madine, count me in, too.

MON MOTHMA: Well said, Leia.

THREEPIO: *(TO LEIA)* While I would not wish to sound presumptuous, Your Highness, I must be included as well. Master Luke would expect no less of me.

LEIA: We couldn't get along without you, Threepio.

HAN: Welcome aboard, Goldenrod.

MADINE: *(FROM OFF)* Solo, by my reckoning that leaves you one officer short for your command crew.

HAN: Right, sir. I was thinking—["—of asking for volunteers after the briefing."]

LUKE: *(FROM OFF)* Han, I'm with you, too.

LEIA: Luke!

THREEPIO: And Artoo-Detoo! Oh, my . . .

ARTOO: PIPES A HELLO, MOVING ON.

CROWD: MUTTERS AND EXCLAMATIONS, WILD LINES, AT LUKE'S SUDDEN AND DRAMATIC APPEARANCE.

HAN: It looks like the roster's complete, General Madine.

MON MOTHMA: Time is short. Moreover, we must adjust our own plans to make up for the losses inflicted on us by Lord Vader at the Battle of the Bajic Shipyards. So let us now conclude the overview briefing and divide into operational groups for final preparation.

Sound: More scraping of chairs, etc., under next.

CROWD: WILD LINES AND COMMENTS AS THE MEETING BREAKS UP.

LEIA: *(TO LUKE AS HE MOVES ON)* Luke—what is it? What's wrong?

LUKE: Ask me that again when we have more time to talk, Leia.

LANDO: Commander Skywalker, you have a dramatic sense of timing.

LUKE: Good to see you, too, Lando.

HAN: Luke, if I was you I would've stayed away a little longer.

LUKE: Hi, Han. Chewie—whoa!

CHEWBACCA: GROWLS AFFECTIONATELY.

LUKE: *(INDICATING THE WOOKIEE BEAR HUG HE'S RECEIVING)* I missed you, too, old timer, but you don't see me cracking your ribs . . .

THREEPIO: Artoo, I trust you've been comporting yourself in a responsible manner.

ARTOO: SINGSONGS A REPLY.

THREEPIO: Unfortunately, our problems aren't over yet.

ARTOO: ANSWERS WITH A RUN OF ELECTRONIC S/FX.

THREEPIO: There are many ways of describing this situation, Artoo, but "exciting" is hardly the word I would choose.

SCENE 4–2 REBEL FRIGATE LAUNCH BAY

Sound: HQ frigate launch bay comes up, with characteristic sounds.

REBEL CONTROLLER: *(BACKGROUND, OVER PA SYSTEM)* Shuttle *Tydirium* preflight check is completed. Troop complement now embarking. Command crew, shuttle *Tydirium*, report to crew stations.

HAN: *(MOVING ON)* Hey, Lando.

LANDO: Yeah?

HAN: Look, I want you to take the *Falcon* on this mission.

LANDO: What!?

HAN: I mean it. You need all the help you can get and she's the fastest ship in the fleet.

LANDO: Thanks, Han. I know what she means to you, old buddy. I'll take good care of her. She . . . she won't get a scratch, all right?

HAN: Right. I got your promise. "Not a scratch."

LANDO: Hey, the *Falcon* used to be mine, remember? I've flown that hunk of junk through more tough spots than you have.

HAN: This one'll be the toughest, Lando.

LANDO: Yeah, what does it look like, I'm fresh off a moisture farm?

HAN: I didn't say that, I just—["—I just want to hear you say you'll bring 'er back in one piece."]

LANDO: We'll be inside the Death Star and blow the reactor before the Empire even realizes we're there . . . assuming you don't mess up. So would you get going, you pirate?

HAN: Clear skies, Lando.

LANDO: Thanks. Good luck, Han.

SCENE 4–3   SHUTTLE *TYDIRIUM* COCKPIT

Sound: Instrumentation sounds of Luke and Chewbacca running more preflight checks.

LUKE: Chewie, that fake clearance code's causing static on the IFF transponder. Give me some signal clarification, would you?

Sound: Chewbacca snapping toggles, etc., under next.

CHEWBACCA: LOWS A DISTRACTED ANSWER AS HE WORKS.

LUKE: Okay, that's got it.

HAN: *(MOVING ON)* You got her warmed up, Luke?

LUKE: Almost, Han. The flight decks on these Imperial shuttles are a little cramped for Chewie, though.

CHEWBACCA: GROWLS IRRITABLY.

HAN: I don't think the Empire had Wookiees in mind when they designed 'em. How's that right hand, Luke? You took a nasty shot back there on Tatooine.

LUKE: It's fine, Han. Fixing a bionic limb's easier than healing flesh and blood, I guess. Being part machine has its advantages.

HAN: Y'know, we've got plenty of spare blasters, Luke. You don't have to limit yourself . . .

LUKE: Thanks anyway, Han, but the lightsaber is the only weapon a Jedi needs.

HAN: Huh.

LUKE: This thing's going to come out right, you'll see. We'll make it come out right.

HAN: Yeah, wish I had the same confidence in the Force that you do.

LUKE: For what it's worth, the Force seems to have confidence in you.

HAN: For some reason, that doesn't make me feel any better.

SCENE 4–4   SHUTTLE *TYDIRIUM* COCKPIT

Sound: Brief transition in time but not location. Tydirium *flight deck comes back up with instrumentation noises but no activity on Han's part.*

LEIA: *(MOVING ON)* Han, hey, are you awake?

HAN: Yeah, just looking at the *Falcon*. Can't shake this funny feeling, like I'm not gonna see her again.

CHEWBACCA: *(SLIGHTLY OFF)* RUMBLES UNHAPPILY.

THREEPIO: *(MOVING ON)* Pardon me, Your Highness. General Solo.

ARTOO: TOOTLES A QUICK UPDATE.

THREEPIO: Artoo says Major Derlin reports his commandos secured for launch.

LEIA: *(TO HAN)* Come on, General. Liftoff time.

HAN: Okay. Chewie, let's see what this bucket of bolts can do. Ready, Luke?

LUKE: All set.

HAN: All right then. Hang on, everybody.

ARTOO: WHISTLES HAPPILY, READY FOR SOME ADVENTURE.

THREEPIO: Yes, Artoo, here we go again.

Sound: Tydirium*'s engines rise as the shuttle lifts off to depart the* *launch bay. During transition, sound of TIE fighters and Star Destroyers helps establish the Imperial presence of the Death Star.*

SCENE 4–5 SHUTTLE *TYDIRIUM* COCKPIT

Sound: Flight deck comes back up, this time with instrumentation very active, especially communications gear.

LEIA: Coming up on their detection perimeter now, Han.

HAN: Cue up the IFF transponder, Chewie. And stay sharp. If the Imperials don't go for this code we're gonna have to get out of here quick.

CHEWBACCA: WOOFS A "WILCO."

THREEPIO: Another Death Star! Just the sight of it has my stress compensators in flux.

LUKE: Steady, Threepio.

ARTOO: SINGSONGS AN ENCOURAGEMENT TO HIS COUNTER-PART.

DEATH STAR CONTROLLER: *(OVER COMMO)* Shuttlecraft, we have you on our screen now. Please identify.

HAN: This is shuttle *Tydirium*, requesting deactivation of the deflector shield.

DS CONTROLLER: Shuttle *Tydirium*, transmit the clearance code for shield passage.

HAN: Transmission commencing. *(TO SLIGHTLY OFF)* Hit it, Chewie.

CHEWBACCA: ACKNOWLEDGES.

Sound: A touchpad is keyed, with resulting tones. The code sequence is transmitted, a high-density data stream.

LEIA: Here's where we find out if that code is worth the price we paid for it.

HAN: It'll work, it'll work.

THREEPIO: Good gracious, look at the size of that capital ship. It must be a hundred times as massive as the rest.

HAN: Super Star Destroyer. What a monster.

LEIA: Luke, what's wrong?

LUKE: Vader's on that ship.

HAN: Now don't get jittery, Luke. There's a lot of command ships. *(TO CHEWBACCA)* Keep your distance though, Chewie. But don't look like you're keeping your distance.

CHEWBACCA: SNARLS "JUST HOW'M I SUPPOSED TO DO THAT?"

HAN: I don't know. Fly casual.

THREEPIO: Would this trickery fall under the definition of "Corellian Overdrive," General Solo?

HAN: Only if it works.

LEIA: They're not responding. They must be passing the clearance up the chain of command.

HAN: Yeah. They're not goin' for it, Chewie.

CHEWBACCA: VENTS HIS ALARM.

LUKE: I can feel Vader's presence. I'm endangering the mission. I shouldn't have come.

HAN: It's your imagination, kid. Let's keep a little optimism, here.

DS CONTROLLER: *(OVER COMMO)* Shuttle *Tydirium*, deactivation of the defensive shield will commence immediately. Maintain your present course.

HAN: Okay. No problem. Told you Vader wasn't around, Luke. You think he'd let us breeze in here if he was?

LUKE: I wonder.

THREEPIO: May we hope, General Solo, that the most perilous part of the journey is over?

HAN: Well, hope away, Threepio. Course, we have to set down without being detected, rig that generator installation to blow, and get out again before the Imperials come down on us. But outside of that, it's gonna be a pleasant little walk in the woods.

THREEPIO: Oh. Oh yes, Endor is said to be a sylvan paradise of sorts, isn't it?

LEIA: That would depend on your definition of paradise.

SCENE 4–6   ENDOR FOREST

Sound: External Endor comes up, with forest sounds, external bird-song and beasties, noises of the file of Rebels moving through the old-growth woods. Also heard are the sounds of Artoo's motors and treads, and Threepio's walking servos.

THREEPIO: *(GRIPING SOTTO VOCE TO HIS COUNTERPART, WHO'S NEAR HIM IN THE LINE OF MARCH)* Sylvan paradise indeed! Hmmph! Watch where you're going, Artoo. This timber-land is difficult enough to negotiate as it is. What good is all this primeval beauty if it's the last thing we ever see?

LUKE: Keep it down, Threepio.

CHEWBACCA: CONCURS SOFTLY.

HAN: *(FROM SLIGHTLY OFF, A STAGE WHISPER)* Hold it up! Everybody hunker down.

THREEPIO: Oh, Artoo, I told you it was dangerous here!

ARTOO: GIVES AN APPREHENSIVE, MUTED RUN OF NOTES.

LUKE: *(IN THE SAME TONE)* What's up, Han?

HAN: Two Imperial scouts. Standing by their speeder bikes down in that clearing, see?

LEIA: Should we try and go around them?

HAN: That'd take time, and this whole party'll be for nothing if they spot us. Chewie and me'll take care of this. You stay here.

LUKE: Take them out quietly, Han. There might be more scouts out there.

HAN: What're you worried about? It's me.

LEIA: Try to have a little confidence, there, Han.

HAN: Sweet! *(TO CHEWBACCA, MOVING OFF, INDICATING EF-FORT OF MOVING FORWARD THROUGH THE FOLIAGE)* C'mon, Chewie. It's nap time for stormtroopers . . .

CHEWBACCA: *(MOVING OFF)* RUMBLES SOFTLY.

LEIA: How can a man go through all the things he has and not learn any humility?

LUKE: Han's only got two modes: frozen stiff in carbonite, and full speed ahead.

SCENE 4–7   EXTERIOR ENDOR

Music: Brief transition, as Han and Chewie work their way into position.

LEIA: *(A STAGE WHISPER)* There're over there, Han and Chewie, behind that tree.

LUKE: Get set to move up fast if they need help.

Sound: (OFF) A twig cracks under Han's boot, clearly audible in the old-growth stillness.

LEIA: Han's foot snapped a twig.

SCOUT #2: *(OFF)* Behind you!

SCOUT #1: *(OFF, TO HAN)* Back off, you! *(INDICATES EFFORT OF KNOCKING HAN BACK AGAINST A TREE)*

HAN: INDICATES SHOCK, PAIN, IMPACT OF THE BLOW.

LUKE: They blew it! C'mon, Leia!

Sound: Noises of Han's dustup with the stormtrooper, under next. Crack and rustle of forest-floor duff, impact of blows to the armored Imperial, etc. POV moves closer to signify Luke and Leia charging to the scene of the action.

HAN & SCOUT #1: INDICATE THE FURIOUS FIGHT. GRUNTS, ETC. MOVE CLOSER TO POV TO SIGNIFY LUKE AND LEIA'S RUSH FORWARD.

SCOUT #1: *(TO OFF)* Get your speeder! Go for help!

SCOUT #2: *(FROM OFF)* Right!

Sound: Scout #2's speeder bike cranks up and wails off at high speed, under next.

LEIA: The other one's getting away.

LUKE: Chewie, shoot him!

CHEWBACCA: ACKNOWLEDGES.

Sound: The twang and laser blast of one of the Wookiee's bow-caster bolts. The energy quarrel streaks off, exploding over speeder bike noises.

SCOUT #2: YELLS IN PAIN AND DISMAY AS HE'S HIT AND CA-REENS FOR A CRASH.

Sound: There are secondary sputters and explosions, followed by the terrific impact of the speeder smacking into a giant hardwood tree. Clatter as debris falls, flames crackle, etc.

LUKE: Got 'im!

LEIA: Luke, to the right! Two more scouts!

Sound: Two more speeder bikes crank up and race off, under next.

LUKE: They're running for it.

LEIA: Here's another speeder bike. We can catch 'em.

Sound: Leia scrambling onto the bike, "kickstarting" it, etc., under next.

LEIA: *(INDICATES GETTING THE FLYING HOG GOING, ETC.)* Can't let them raise the alarm.

LUKE: Leia, wait! I'm coming with you!

LEIA: C'mon!

Sound: Luke hastily hops on behind her.

LUKE: *(INDICATING THE EXERTION OF CLIMBING ABOARD)* Wait for me!

LEIA: Hang on, Luke!

Sound: Speeder revs, zooms off in a burst of engine power that echoes in the cathedral of tree trunks.

HAN: *(OFF, VOICE FADING SHARPLY AS THEIR POV MOVES AWAY FROM HIM AT SPEED)* Luke! Leia! Wait!

LUKE: Quick, jam their comlink. That center switch.

Sound: A toggle being thrown, ripple of high, streaming blips signifies communications jamming.

LEIA: Got it, but we still have to stop those riders from sounding the alarm.

106

LUKE: Watch out for that branch!

Sound: The speeder whoops as she maneuvers. They Doppler past a low-hanging limb.

LUKE: REACTS.

LEIA: REACTS.

LUKE: Gun it!

LEIA: D'you drive as well from the front seat, Luke?

LUKE: Watch out!

Sound: Howl of speeder, slap of leaves as they crash through a screen of branches.

LEIA: *(REACTS TO THE BREAKTHROUGH, THEN SPITS OUT LEAF BITS, TWIGS, ETC.)* Gahh!

LUKE: Move up—*(SPITS DEBRIS, TOO)*—up alongside the one who's falling behind! Bump him if you can!

Sound: The speeder yowls. Leia starts playing bumper cars against the side of the trailing Imperial bike, under next.

LEIA: Why?

LUKE: I'm gonna jump him. Ready? *(REACTS TO BUMPING)*

LEIA: *(REACTS TO THE SADDLEBAG JOUSTING)* Wait . . . wait . . . awright, now!

Sound: Speeders grazing each other, labor of engines, collision of Luke with the armored scout, under next.

LUKE: INDICATES A LEAP FROM THE PILLION SEAT OF ONE SPEEDER TO THAT OF THE OTHER, POUNCING ON SCOUT #3.

SCOUT #3: *(VOICE PROCESSED TO SIGNIFY HELMET SPEAKER, REACTS)* Get off me, you filthy scum—

LUKE: INDICATES CLOBBERING THE SCOUT AND FLIPPING HIM OUT OF THE SADDLE.

Sound: Speeder sounds convey lack of control, rattles and impacts signify struggle. Scout's fall ends in an armored splat against a tree, during next.

SCOUT #3: REACTS TO BLOW AND BEING UNSEATED, VOICE FADING AS LUKE'S POV MOVES AWAY FROM HIM. INDICATES TERMINAL IMPACT WITH UNPROPITIOUSLY SITUATED TREE.

LEIA: *(FROM OFF, STILL CONNING HER BIKE)* You all right, Luke?

LUKE: Fine, but we've got to get that other scout.

LEIA: With two of us we ought to be able to box him in.

LUKE: Yeah, if the trees don't get us all first.

Sound: They race their speeders through the resounding, bosky spaces. Suddenly, light blaster cannon shots range in on them from astern in near-misses, exploding against tree trunks, etc.

LEIA: Who's shooting at us?

LUKE: Two more Imperials, right on our tail.

Sound: More shots from behind. One glances off Luke's bike.

LUKE: *(REACTS)* Keep after that one. I'll take the two behind us.

LEIA: Good luck!

Sound: Her speeder revs as she accelerates to overtake her quarry. More threading among the titan trees. Another volley of shots mew in at Luke from his pursuers.

LUKE: *(REACTS) (TO HIMSELF, AS IF HE'S TALKING TO THE IMPE-RIALS)* All right, let's find out how good you boys are at sudden stops . . .

Sound: The blast of retro thrusters, complaint of the bike's power plant, as Luke suddenly decelerates. One-and-two, the bandits on his tail go zooming past to either side, unable to compensate for his maneuver.

LUKE: *("TO THE SCOUT" BUT ACTUALLY TO HIMSELF)* Not good. Overshot me!

Sound: Luke gooses his engine, accelerates hard.

LUKE: *(INDICATING HE'S CONNING THE SPEEDER FOR ALL IT'S WORTH)* How do you guys like it in the hot seat? *(INDICATES FIR-ING HIS SPEEDER'S LIGHT CANNON)*

Sound: Cannon fires. More sounds of passage among the trees.

LUKE: No matter how you jostle each other, boys, one of you's gonna end up in the crosshairs . . . *(INDICATES FIRING AGAIN)*

Sound: Brief fusillade from Luke's gun. One round finds its target, extreme off, sending an Imperial out of control head-on into the trunk of a forest giant. Sound whips past Luke's POV as he continues the chase.

LUKE: One down, one to go. But where'd he disappear to— *(RE-ACTS TO NEXT)*

Sound: The remaining Imperial chopper veers in at Luke, blindsiding him in a collision.

109

LUKE: Time to bail out! *(INDICATES A DESPERATE LEAP TO GET CLEAR BEFORE HIS SPEEDER HITS A TREE)*

Sound: Blowup and accompanying racket of the speeder's destruction.

LUKE: *(PANTING, SHAKEN, ETC., FROM FALL AND AWARENESS THAT HE'S THE QUARRY AGAIN)* Whew. Luke on foot, trooper on bike . . . not good, not good.

Sound: The other speeder circling, off, for an attack run at Luke.

LUKE: Okay, Jedi. As Han would say, "Show 'em what you've got."

Sound: Click of Luke unhooking his lightsaber from his belt. Ignition switch flicks, lightsaber hisses to moaning, crackling life.

LUKE: Any time you're ready, trooper . . .

Sound: The enemy speeder's closing on him. Its shots come shrieking in, detonating to either side, blowing apart bark and brush, etc. Luke deflects several shots with his lightsaber, saber sounds mingling with laser blasts.

LUKE: *(INDICATES EFFORT OF DEFLECTING SPEEDER BOLTS)*

Sound: The speeder's almost on top of him. Shots peppering the air.

LUKE: *(INDICATES THE ACT OF A TREMENDOUS, FLAWLESSLY TIMED STROKE OF THE BLADE, A TOTAL EFFORT)* Let the Force . . . guide my stroke . . . now!

Sound: Lightsaber slashes through metal as blaster bolts thunder. The outcome is lost in the rise of music for transition.

SCENE 4–8 ENDOR EXTERIOR

Sound: Another part of the forest comes up, Han and the rest in the clearing where things first went awry.

HAN: *(TO OFF)* Hey, Threepio! Tell Major Derlin to set up a com-link surveillance. Maybe if that jamming stops we can eavesdrop on the Imperial frequencies.

THREEPIO: At once, sir—oh! General Solo, someone is coming. It's Master Luke!

LUKE: *(FROM OFF)* Han!

HAN: *(TO OFF)* Hey, Luke, where's Leia?

LUKE: *(MOVING ON)* What? She didn't come back?

HAN: I thought she was with you.

LUKE: No, we got separated.

ARTOO: DOES A QUICK OCARINA-RUN OF EXPOSITION.

THREEPIO: Sirs, Artoo just informed me that the jamming stopped a short while ago, but there has been no comlink response from the princess, yet.

LUKE: It was Leia doing the jamming. Han, we'd better go look for her.

HAN: Right. You and me, with Chewie to do the tracking. Three-pio, tell Derlin that we'll rendezvous at the shield generator.

LUKE: I'll get Chewie.

THREEPIO: General Solo.

HAN: What?

THREEPIO: I strongly suggest you allow Artoo and me to come as well. You'll need Artoo's scanners for the search.

LUKE: He's got a point, Han.

HAN: *(MOVING OFF)* You're on, Threepio.

LUKE: *(MOVING OFF)* Be ready to move fast, you two.

THREEPIO: *(TO LUKE, OFF)* Don't worry, Master Luke. We know what to do.

ARTOO: VOUCHES FOR THAT.

THREEPIO: *(TO ARTOO)* And you said it was "pretty" here. Ugh!

ARTOO: PIPES AN INTERROGATIVE.

THREEPIO: No, my idea of paradise would be a coronation ceremony held in a cybernetics clean-room. Oh, well. Artoo, prepare to move in high gear.

SCENE 4–9   ENDOR FOREST CLEARING

Sound: Another part of the Endor forest. A breeze, or different animal calls, signify the change in locale.

LEIA: MOANS, BEGINNING TO RESUME CONSCIOUSNESS [AFTER BEING KNOCKED COLD, HAVING BEEN FLUNG TO THE GROUND WHEN HER SPEEDER WAS SHOT DOWN BY THE LAST SCOUT—WHO IN TURN SELF-DESTRUCTED A MOMENT LATER AS HIS OWN BIKE HIT YET ANOTHER TREE].

WICKET: THE EWOK IS MAKING A WARY-BUT-CURIOUS CHIT-TER, OFF.

LEIA: *(MOANS AGAIN)* What . . . where am I?

WICKET: JABBERS TO HIMSELF AS HE MOVES ON. [VOICE SHOULD INDICATE ACTIVITY—HE'S PRODDING LEIA WITH SPEAR.]

LEIA: *(STILL HALF OUT OF IT)* Stop . . . stop poking me. *(ROUS-ING SOMEWHAT)* I said cut it out— *(STARTLED, WAKING TO THE SIGHT OF HIM)* Whoa!

WICKET: JUMPS BACK, BRISTLING AT HER.

LEIA: What in blazes are you?

WICKET: GROWLS WARNINGLY.

LEIA: You can lower that spear, little fella. I'm not gonna hurt you. See? No need to get your fur all ruffled.

WICKET: GRUMBLES, BUT IS MOLLIFIED.

LEIA: *(GRUNTS AND GROANS A BIT MORE, FEELING HER IN-JURIES)* Last thing I remember, that Imperial shot me down, then punched his speeder into a tree.

WICKET: TRIES TO HOLD UP HIS END OF THE CONVERSATION.

LEIA: Looks like I'm stuck here. Trouble is, I don't know where here is. Maybe you can help me.

WICKET: SAYS WHAT THEY HAVE IS A FAILURE TO COMMUNICATE.

LEIA: *(INDICATES SHIFTING TO SIT ON A LOG)* Come on, sit down over here by me.

Sound: She pats the log.

WICKET: CHATTERS MORE AMIABLY AS HE MOVES TO HER SIDE.

113

LEIA: That's it. I promise I won't hurt you.

WICKET: INDICATES TAKING A SEAT NEXT TO HER.

LEIA: Our reports didn't say Endor had intelligent life-forms. You look well fed, I'll say that for you. Want something to eat?

Sound: She unsnaps a belt pouch, unwraps an emergency ration stick, under next.

LEIA: How about a ration bar? *(MAKES NIBBLING, LIP-SMACKING NOISES, ETC., TO GET THE IDEA ACROSS)* Mmm, good, see?

WICKET: PROFOUNDLY INTERESTED IN A NEW GUSTATORIAL EXPERIENCE.

LEIA: That's right. Here, take it.

WICKET: HESITATES, THEN GOES FOR IT.

Sound: Wicket discarding the wrapper, sniffing the food, licking and nibbling to sample it, then piling in, chomping away, under next.

LEIA: That's it. Just let me get rid of this helmet and maybe I can—["take a better look around this place, get my bearings."]

WICKET: GOBBLES IN ALARM AT THE SIGHT, JUMPING BACK FROM HER. INDICATES ACT OF SCRAMBLING AWAY.

LEIA: What? It's just a hat. It's not going to hurt you. My, you are a jittery little thing, aren't you?

WICKET: ANSWERING JABBER STOPS IN MIDSYLLABLE. HE STARTS SNIFFING THE AIR, HAVING SMELLED/HEARD ENEMIES.

LEIA: What is it? Is someone coming?

Sound: A blaster bolt mews by, exploding near Leia.

LEIA: *(INDICATING SHE'S DIVING FOR COVER)* Take cover!

WICKET: BLEATS AND CHITTERS IN FEAR, MOVING OFF.

Sound: Another sniper round zings in.

LEIA: *(STAGE WHISPER)* Keep your head down— Hey, where'd you go? *(WHISTLES FOR HIM SOFTLY)* Endorian?

SCOUT #1: *(HAVING SNEAKED UP ON HER POV)* Freeze, or I'll fire!

LEIA: Okay, okay, don't shoot.

SCOUT #1: Hand over the blaster.

LEIA: Here— *(INDICATES GIVING IT UP AS HE SNATCHES IT AWAY ROUGHLY)*

Sound: Clatter of the sidearm against the scout's gauntlet.

SCOUT #1: *(INDICATES GRABBING THE GUN)* Right. *(TO OFF)* Unit 4, go get your speeder and take the prisoner back to the base.

SCOUT #4: *(FROM OFF)* Yes, sir!

SCOUT #1: *(TO LEIA)* And you, don't move a muscle or—["—you won't get there in very good condition."]

WICKET: GROWLS AND THREATENS, PINKING THE GUY WITH HIS SPEAR.

SCOUT #1: Oww! What the creeping crawling—["—bloody blazes is stabbing my leg?"]

LEIA: Sorry, Private— *(INDICATES EFFORT OF SWINGING A PIECE OF FALLEN BRANCH AT HIM)*

Sound: Leia's club smacking the scout's helmet.

SCOUT #1: GROANS, ETC.

LEIA: *("TO HIM" BUT ACTUALLY TO HERSELF)* —but here's where we part company.

WICKET: GABBLES IN ELATION.

LEIA: Thanks, little guy. Stay down, I've gotta stop the other one.

Sound: Leia fumbles for and recovers her pistol. Speeder bike cranks up, off.

LEIA: *(INDICATES FIRING HER PISTOL)* Look out, fella!

Sound: Leia's laser pistol fires rapidly. Speeder sounds are mixed with shots registering, off. Speeder screams out of control and smashes into a tree, under next.

SCOUT #4: *(SHOUTS HIS LAST, AS HE HEAD-ONS INTO THE TREE, OFF)*

LEIA: Got 'im . . . At least the Empire hasn't gotten the alarm yet.

WICKET: REJOICES IN THE VICTORY. SPEAKS URGENTLY.

LEIA: If you're saying we've got to get out of here fast, I'm with you, little guy. Lead the way.

WICKET: *(MOVING OFF)* KEEPS UP THE PATTER AS HE GUIDES HER AWAY FROM THE SCENE.

LEIA: Y'know, you're looking better to me all the time, Short, Round, and Furry.

Sound: Transition, as forest scene fades to background.

NARRATOR: Among the Rebels, pathways have begun to diverge, as friends part company on their separate missions. While Han and Luke wait anxiously for Leia's return, Lando Calrissian prepares for a daring assault on the Death Star, his fortunes depending entirely on the success of his friends' mission to destroy the shield generator. In their hands rests the fate of billions, as the Rebellion struggles toward ultimate victory or utter defeat. And all the while, in the throne room of his mighty battle station, the Emperor watches, and waits.

Music: Closing theme up under credits.

NARRATOR: CLOSING CREDITS.

EPISODE FIVE:
"SO TURNS A GALAXY,
SO TURNS A WHEEL"

CAST:
Emperor Palpatine
Darth Vader
Han
Luke
Threepio
Leia
Imperial Commander
Imperial Scout #1
Imperial Scout #2
Major Derlin

SOUND/FX ROLES:
Artoo-Detoo
Chewbacca
Ewoks
Teebo
Vine Ewok
Logray
Cub Ewok
Wicket
Paploo

ANNOUNCER: OPENING CREDITS.

Music: Opening theme.

NARRATOR: A long time ago in a galaxy far, far away there came a time of revolution, when Rebels united to challenge a tyrannical Empire. After decades of conflict and war, the vast struggle is about to play itself to a conclusion on and around the idyllic forest moon of the planet Endor. The Rebels' makeshift armada is on its way to attack the Empire's new Death Star, but its success depends on a fearless expeditionary force far below on the forest moon, which is struggling to deactivate the defensive shield protecting the battle station. But their plans are not as secret as they would wish. The Rebels' every move has been foreseen by their greatest adversary, the Emperor Palpatine. Now, waiting in his throne room, he looks to the servant, and the conquest, that will gain him more power than any mere military victory could provide.

SCENE 5-1 EMPEROR'S ROOM ON DEATH STAR

Sound: A heavy, powered chamber door slides open.

EMPEROR: *(TO OFF)* Enter. Enter, my friend.

Sound: Vader's breathing apparatus and measured bootsteps move on.

EMPEROR: It is always good to see my strong right arm.

VADER: Thank you, my master. I bow before you in obedience.

EMPEROR: Obedience, you say. Yet, I told you to remain on the command ship, to carry out my orders.

VADER: A small Rebel infiltration force has penetrated our energy shields and landed on the Sanctuary Moon of Endor.

EMPEROR: I am aware of it.

VADER: My son is with them.

EMPEROR: Are you certain?

VADER: I have felt him, my master.

EMPEROR: Strange, that I have not. I wonder if your feelings on this matter are clear, Lord Vader.

VADER: They are clear, my master. But I sense that Skywalker has grown strong in the Force.

EMPEROR: That is of no significance to me. Go to the Sanctuary Moon and wait for him. When he comes, bring him here before me.

VADER: As you wish, my master.

EMPEROR: Even so. And here, I shall either make Skywalker my own or I shall destroy him.

SCENE 5-2   ENDOR FOREST

Sound: The same woodland clearing in which Leia fought for her life and met Wicket. Animal calls, "bird" song, branches creaking in the breeze, and leaves rustling, etc. Sound of droids' servos, twigs cracking, and duff gritting underfoot, etc., as the Rebels search the area.

HAN: *(TO OFF)* Luke! Luke, get over here!

LUKE: *(MOVING ON)* What is it, Han? Did you find Leia?

THREEPIO: Oh, Master Luke. If only we had.

HAN: No, but her speeder's behind that fallen tree, totaled.

LUKE: There's two more wrecked speeders back there. And I found her helmet.

HAN: Leia must still be alive. It's the only explanation.

THREEPIO: I'm afraid that Artoo's sensors can find no trace of the princess in this vicinity.

ARTOO: PIPES SADLY.

LUKE: What about Chewie? Can't he track her?

CHEWBACCA: VENTS HIS FRUSTRATION, OFF, TRYING TO PICK UP HER TRAIL.

HAN: He says something else has been here. Something besides stormtroopers. Whatever it was, it left no tracks when it moved on and Chewie thinks it covered Leia's, too.

THREEPIO: Oh dear. You mean, something is stalking the princess?

LUKE: That doesn't make sense. Why would—["—a predator or a hunter bother to cover Leia's tracks?"]

CHEWBACCA: HALLOOS, OFF, TO TELL THEM HE'S ON TO SOMETHING.

HAN: *(TO OFF)* What? Chewie, what?

LUKE: Let's go see.

Sound: The two men and the two droids moving through undergrowth, etc., under next.

HAN: *(INDICATING MAKING HIS WAY THROUGH THE BUSH)* He says he's picked up a scent. Over here.

LUKE: *(NEGOTIATING THROUGH BRACKEN)* He's right, there's something there.

CHEWBACCA: TRUMPETS HIS SUCCESS.

LUKE: I think he's found it.

HAN: *(INDICATES HE'S EMERGED FROM THE SCRUB)* What the— Hey, what is this thing? I don't get it.

THREEPIO: It would appear to be an animal carcass hung from a wooden pole.

ARTOO: HAZARDS A GUESS.

THREEPIO: Someone's lunch? If it is, it doesn't say much for their appreciation of the fine dining experience.

CHEWBACCA: SNUFFLES AT THE CARCASS, THEN VOICES A QUESTION TO HAN.

HAN: Naw, I don't wanna taste it.

LUKE: *(SENSING SOMETHING'S WRONG)* Chewbacca, step away from it.

CHEWBACCA: GROWLS TRUCULENTLY.

LUKE: No, don't touch it. Chewie, wait! Do-ooon't! *(REACTS TO THE TRAP BEING SPRUNG)*

Sound: A crude wooden trigger mechanism is tripped, releasing ropes of twisted grass that whip through the air, then twang as they come under tension. The net trap concealed under the forest floor mulch is yanked up, catching them all. Heavier cable sings and saws against the limb above as the net's hauled into the air by a deadweight, under next. Smaller twigs and branches, either broken off or shaken loose from the snare, fall to the ground. Sequence ends with the "purse string" rope creaking and rubbing slowly against the limb, as the net swings like a lazy pendulum.

HAN: It's a trap! *(REACTS TO BEING BAGGED AND HOISTED)*

THREEPIO: *(REACTS)* Oh-hh!

ARTOO: BEEPS IN DISTRESS.

HAN: *(INDICATES STRAIN OF HANGING IN THE BAG, PRESSED UP AGAINST THE OTHERS, UNABLE TO STRUGGLE MUCH AND THAT, INEFFECTUALLY)* Nice work, Chewie! You got us snared in a net trap!

THREEPIO: One would suppose a two-hundred-year-old Wook-iee to have learned a measure of self-restraint.

CHEWBACCA: BELATEDLY, ABJECTLY SORRY.

HAN: Great! Always thinking with your stomach!

LUKE: *(ALSO INDICATING PRESSURES OF CAPTIVITY)* Will you take it easy? Let's just figure a way to get out of this oversize string bag. Han, can you reach my lightsaber?

HAN: 'Course I can. *(STRAINS, UNSUCCESSFULLY)* No problem. *(TRIES HARDER, TO NO AVAIL)* Be right with you . . .

ARTOO: BLEEPS STAUNCHLY THAT HE'S GOT THE SOLUTION.

THREEPIO: Artoo, what do you mean, you'll "handle this?"

Sound: A port pops open in Artoo's fuselage and a servo-powered appendage extends, clicking into place. That done, Artoo's mini-buzzsaw revs up, under next.

THREEPIO: Artoo, I'm not sure that cutting the bottom of the net open with your circular saw is at all a good idea.

HAN: What's he doin'?

Sound: Net strands parting, other rope starting to rip, net joinings giving way, etc., under next.

THREEPIO: After all, Artoo, from up here it's a very long drooop! *(REACTS TO FALL)*

LUKE: REACTS.

HAN: REACTS.

CHEWBACCA: BAYS IN CONSTERNATION.

ARTOO: COMBINATION "YOW!" AND "WAHOO!"

Sound: Men, automatons, and Wookiee thud to the forest floor, knocking into each other as well.

CHEWBACCA: GRUNTS IN PAIN, REGRETTING HIS FOLLY.

Sound: Rustling of the leaves and bushes as the Ewoks move in, under next.

HAN: Me, too, Chewie. Must've hit my head—is it my imagination or are the bushes moving?

LUKE: It's not your imagination, Han.

EWOKS: CHATTER AND COMMOTION.

HAN: What in the starry-eyed universe are those things?

CHEWBACCA: GROWLS IN HOSTILITY AND WARNING.

TEEBO: GABBLES, TELLING THEM THEY'RE PRISONERS.

HAN: Hey, point that spear someplace else, ya furry butterball!

LUKE: Han, no blasters! They've got us covered from all sides.

EWOKS: OMINOUS MUTTERINGS.

HAN: Captured by a pack of stone-axe-wavin' gremlins. I'm never gonna live this down— *(REACTING TO NEXT)*

Sound: Indicative clacking and so on, under next, as weapons are confiscated. Retaining strap on Han's holster unsnapped, Luke's lightsaber belt ring unclipped from his belt, etc.

LUKE: Calm down, Han. It'll be all right. Here, you can have my lightsaber.

HAN: Awright. *(TO EWOK)* Here, take the gun.

Sound: Weapon clatters a bit as it's passed over, under next.

HAN: Chewie, give 'em your bowcaster.

CHEWBACCA: MOANS UNHAPPILY, COMPLYING.

Sound: Rattle of the laser crossbow weapon being surrendered, its shoulder-strap buckle clinking, etc.

LUKE: Artoo, where's Threepio? We need a translator.

ARTOO: GIVES A WHISTLE, TRYING TO GET AN ANSWER FROM THREEPIO.

LUKE: I think he landed in those ferns.

Sound: Attendant racket of Threepio sitting up, chassis clacking and woodsy noises.

THREEPIO: *(GROANS, OFF, INDICATING CYBERNETIC-ANALOG "PAIN" OF THE FALL, EFFORT TO SIT BACK UPRIGHT, DISORIENTA-TION)* Oh, my head! What a nerve-shattering plunge! My equilib-rium compensators are—["still spinning."] *(SEEING THE EWOKS)* Oh my goodness!

EWOKS: MASS GASP AS THEY SIGHT THE GOLDEN, IDOL-LIKE THREEPIO. THE INDIGS BEGIN TO CHATTER URGENTLY BUT REVERENTLY TO EACH OTHER, UNDER NEXT.

THREEPIO: Gracious, Master Luke, who are these rotund, hir-sute little beings?

HAN: That's what you're supposed to be telling us.

THREEPIO: I shall inquire, sir. *(TO EWOKS)* <Treetoe doggra. Ee soyoto ambuna nocka.>

EWOKS: TEEBO AND THE OTHERS SHARE EXCITED COM-MENTS.

LUKE: Threepio, do you understand anything they're saying?

THREEPIO: Oh, yes, Master Luke. Remember, I am fluent in over six million forms of communica—

HAN: What're you telling them?

THREEPIO: "Hello," I think. I could be mistaken. These creatures seem to call themselves "Ewoks."

LUKE: Ewoks.

HAN: What're they all bowing and crooning to you for, Goldenrod?

THREEPIO: They're using a very primitive dialect, but I do believe they think I am some sort of god.

ARTOO: GIGGLES AT THE VERY IDEA.

CHEWBACCA: WOOFS DERISIVELY.

LUKE: CAN'T HELP BUT CHUCKLE, TOO.

HAN: Well, why don't you use your divine influence and get us out of this mess?

THREEPIO: I beg your pardon, General Solo, but that just wouldn't be proper.

HAN: "Proper?"

THREEPIO: It's against my programming to impersonate a deity.

CHEWBACCA: SNARLS AT THE CAVILING.

HAN: *(INDICATING THAT HE'S ABOUT TO TROUNCE THREEPIO)* No problem, I'll just open you up right here and do a little field modification on ya—

EWOKS: VOICE THEIR ANGER AS THEY MENACE HIM WITH SPEARS FOR BLASPHEMY.

LUKE: Easy, Han. A stone arrowhead will kill you just as dead as a blaster.

HAN: *(REACTING TO SPEAR JABS)* Ouch! Hey, sorry, boys. My mistake. He's an old friend of mine.

TEEBO: DECLAIMS A PLAN OF ACTION TO HIS COMRADES.

EWOKS: MOTION CARRIED BY UNANIMOUS VOICE VOTE. THEY CHATTER AND COORDINATE AMONG THEMSELVES AS THEY SET TO WORK, UNDER NEXT.

Sound: Ewoks start chopping branches, assembling parts for their carry-poles and Threepio's sedan-chair throne, under next.

LUKE: What're they doing, Threepio?

THREEPIO: Teebo, the war party leader, has decided to take us back to their village. They are building a sedan chair on which I will ride and—sorry to say, sir—carry poles on which they will lash you and the others.

ARTOO: DOESN'T COTTON TO THE IDEA AT ALL.

CHEWBACCA: A BELLIGERENT ROAR.

HAN: Nobody's tying me to a pole.

LUKE: Han, the whole Death Star attack's riding on what we do now.

HAN: Awright, awright. But I don't have to like it . . . Hey, watch it, will ya!

SCENE 5-3   EWOK VILLAGE EXTERIOR

Sound: Signal horn(s) being blown in the distance, drums, Ewoks calling from varying degrees of off, etc.

THREEPIO: A village in the treetops! Isn't this splendid? Wooden bridges in the air and homes carved from tree trunks. Oh, how quaint, that Ewok's traveling on a swinging vine.

VINE EWOK: GOES SAILING PAST, CALLING OUT TO THEM.

HAN: *(INDICATING BEING LUGGED ALONG SUSPENDED BY HIS LASHED WRISTS AND ANKLES)* The view's less impressive for those of us hangin' upside-down, O Almighty Talkingbox.

EWOKS: THEIR WORK CHANTS AND CHATTER CEASE AS THEY REACH THEIR DESTINATION.

LUKE: *(ALSO BEING TOTED BELLY-UP)* What now, Threepio?

THREEPIO: We've reached the village square, Master Luke. Our fate is to be decided by Logray, the village shaman.

EWOKS: DOING A HEAVE-HO CHANT AS THEY SET HAN'S POLE OVER THE BARBECUE PIT.

HAN: What's goin' on? Why're they proppin' me over a fire pit, Threepio?

THREEPIO: I have no idea. Shall I ask, sir?

HAN: I have a really bad feeling about this.

LUKE: Threepio, who's this coming?

Sound: Logray's ceremonial rattle, click-stick, under next.

LOGRAY: *(MOVING ON)* ADDRESSES THE EWOKS AND CAPTIVES, UNDER NEXT.

THREEPIO: That, sir, is Logray, the shaman.

LOGRAY: COMMENTS TO THREEPIO.

THREEPIO: As I understand it, sir, the forest has been invaded by stormtroopers. The Ewoks presume you to be enemies. *(TO LOGRAY)* Excuse me. <Ab toyam, nowb. Ab toyam, no. Hud, ha toy. Ee cotra popeeya.>

LOGRAY: MAKES A GENERAL ANNOUNCEMENT.

HAN: What's he saying?

THREEPIO: I'm rather embarrassed, General Solo, but it appears you are to be the main course at a banquet in my honor.

EWOKS: GIVE FESTIVE AND HUNGRY APPROVAL.

CHEWBACCA: SNARLS IN SURPRISE AND HOSTILITY.

Music: Ewok chanting and drums strike up.

THREEPIO: And you, Artoo, are to be reclaimed for usable scrap.

ARTOO: A SHORT BURST OF OUTRAGE.

THREEPIO: Don't blame me. That's how Logray phrased it.

HAN: So, Luke . . . time to get undiplomatic yet?

LUKE: There's always time for that, Han.

HAN: Only if you're captured by vegetarians.

LEIA: *(MOVING ON)* Han? Luke? What're you doing here?

LUKE: Leia!

HAN: Hey! Princess! I see you finally let your hair down. Looks good.

LEIA: *(TO EWOKS)* Teebo, Logray, this is all a misunderstanding. *(TO TEEBO AND OTHER EWOKS)* Teebo, you've got to release them.

EWOKS: WARNING SNARLS AND MURMURS AS THEY BLOCK HER FROM JOINING HER COMPANIONS.

LUKE: Stay back, Leia.

LEIA: *(REACTS TO SPEARS THRUST HER WAY)* Teebo, no. Put the spears down.

HAN: Back away, Leia, before you end up on the buffet table, too.

LEIA: Logray, these are my friends. Threepio, tell him Luke, Han, and the others must be set free.

THREEPIO: <Roke ta toe-toe. In nee chandu toma tiktik. Ree peetah bah.>

LOGRAY: YAMMERS BACK OBSTINATELY, THEN EXHORTS THE TROOPS.

EWOKS: EXULT, THEN SET TO WORK FEEDING THE COOKING FIRE.

Sound: Wood thrown on the cooking pit blaze, and the flames crackling higher and hotter, under next.

HAN: Somehow, I get the feeling that didn't help us very much.

LEIA: They're stoking up the cooking fire.

LUKE: Threepio, tell them if they don't do as you command, you'll become angry and use your magic.

THREEPIO: But Master Luke, what magic? I couldn't possibly ["—manifest such powers if the Ewoks challenged that assertion."]

LUKE: Just tell them.

THREEPIO: <Horomee ana fu, toron togosh! Toron Togosh! Terro way. Qee t'woos twotoe ai. U wee de dozja. Boom!>

EWOKS: ARE INTIMIDATED BY THE ULTIMATUM.

HAN: Uh, Luke, aren't you even going to watch what happens?

LEIA: Don't distract him, Han. He's calling on the Force.

HAN: He'd better, 'cause Logray's not buying it. And those *(BLOWS ON THE FLAMES CREEPING NEARER)* flames are already at "charbroil" temperature. *(BLOWS SOME MORE)*

LOGRAY: CALLS THREEPIO'S BLUFF.

THREEPIO: You see, Master Luke? They didn't believe me.

LUKE: *(CONCENTRATING ON THE FORCE)* The gravity that holds is a tenuous bond. A bond that can be loosened.

THREEPIO: Just as I said they wouldn't. *(REACTING TO BEING LEVITATED BY LUKE'S FORCE POWERS)* Wait! What's happening to me? I'm floating—floating into the air.

EWOKS: MASS INTAKE OF BREATH AT THE MIRACLE.

THREEPIO: *(OFF, AS HE FLOATS, UNDER NEXT)* Don't let me float away! Get me down! Help! Somebody, help! Master Luke, Artoo! Quickly! I'm floating toward the edge of the platform!

HAN: *(STAGE WHISPER)* Luke, you are the one doing this, aren'tcha?

LEIA: *(STAGE WHISPER)* Hush. Let him concentrate.

THREEPIO: *(OFF, FLOATING)* Help! If I fall from this height there won't be enough left of me to make a hydrospanner!

LUKE: *(STILL IN SEMI-TRANCE)* When the Force warrants, even gravity yields.

EWOKS: SET UP A FRIGHTENED COMMOTION THAT BREAKS INTO THE VENERATION CHANT AGAIN.

LOGRAY: YELLS HYSTERICALLY TO HIS PEOPLE, CONVINCED.

HAN: This is it . . .

LEIA: No—they're releasing you, see?

HAN: Remind me to ask Luke later if he can do that with dice.

LUKE: Gravity enfolds you again, Threepio. Gently . . . down you come.

THREEPIO: *(MOVING ON AS HE'S LOWERED)* Oh, oh, oh! Thank the maker! Some sanity's returning to the laws of nature!

HAN: Hey, you whatchamacallits—Ewoks! Untie these things, and move smartly! *(TO LEIA)* Leia, tell the one who's untying Artoo to be careful. He's still miffed about this whole thing.

ARTOO: DOES AN ANGRY RUN OF TONES, ENDING IN A SHARP, CRACKLING DISCHARGE AS HE ZAPS THE LUCKLESS EWOK IN THE FANNY.

EWOK: YELPS IN PAIN AND FRIGHT, MOVING RAPIDLY OFF.

LEIA: Artoo, that's enough.

ARTOO: STILL COMBATIVE, BUT HE RELENTS.

LUKE: Well done, Threepio.

THREEPIO: I . . . never knew I had it in me, Master Luke.

LUKE: You squelched the sacrifice. Now let's see if you can get the Ewoks on our side.

THREEPIO: But I'm not really programmed for propaganda or political agitation, sir.

LUKE: We just need you to do what you do best, Threepio. Translate the words; tell the story.

THREEPIO: Tell the story? Why, sir, that would be a distinct pleasure.

SCENE 5-4   EWOK VILLAGE INTERIOR

Sound: Drums, music, singing, signal horns, etc. Crackle of a council fire.

EWOKS: MURMURING AMONG THEMSELVES, AS THREEPIO TELLS THE TALE.

THREEPIO: <Ku channa ma fu atta! Ku channa ma fu attas.>

HAN: *(SOTTO VOCE)* Threepio can really pack a house, huh?

LEIA: *(SOTTO VOCE)* There are representatives here from every community in the region.

THREEPIO: *(UNDER NEXT)* <Aranda bo toe toe tafni coroway manna coo-too. Princess Leia wasi weba Artoo. Ooss, vu tata rundi Darth Vader.>

Sound: Threepio re-creates Vader's respiration sounds.

LUKE: *(SOTTO VOCE)* Got enough legroom there, Chewie?

CHEWBACCA: *(AS SOTTO AS HIS VOCE CAN MANAGE)* SAYS IT'LL DO.

THREEPIO: <Un chenko vass qeemo keenan tundi Death Star.>

Sound: A TIE fighter's howl, the blasts of a deep-space dogfight, ending with a modest explosion.

EWOKS: MAKE SOUNDS OF UNCERTAINTY.

THREEPIO: Hmm, let me rephrase that. <Un chenko vass qeemo gogh miyami Death Star.>

Sound: This time Threepio throws in a major blowup.

EWOKS: RATTLED, THRILLED, AND FRIGHTENED BY THE S/FX.

THREEPIO: Ah; that's much more like it.

HAN: *(SOTTO VOCE)* Kinda handy to have a storyteller who makes his own sound effects, huh?

THREEPIO: <Jinachu chaypi kwati . . . ahem, See-Threepio.>

EWOKS: A CONCERTED "AHHH!" AT HEARING THREEPIO IS FRONT AND CENTER IN THE SAGA.

ARTOO: AN ANGRY TRILL.

THREEPIO: I certainly am not "self-aggrandizing," you intrusive little dustbin. Am I, Master Luke?

LUKE: You're doing fine, Threepio.

EWOKS: REACTIONS, UNDER NEXT.

THREEPIO: *(ADDRESSING HIS AUDIENCE AGAIN)* <Ooss, me-chee un Jedi, Obi-Wan Kenobi, ee manna machu Vader con yum yum.>

Sound: A lightsaber ignites and moans.

ARTOO: ARTOO BEGINS INDIGNANT PROTESTS, UNDER NEXT.

THREEPIO: <U tabe—> Yes, Artoo. I was just coming to that. *(GOES BACK TO HIS AUDIENCE)* <Toron togosh.>

Sound: Threepio inserts sounds of troop-carrier AT-ATs, as per the Hoth battle.

THREEPIO: <Master Luke a chimminay choo do-ooo!>

Sound: Threepio dubs in snow speeder making a firing run on the AT-AT, ending in an explosion.

THREEPIO: <Uta *Millennium Falcon* a chimminay Cloud City.>

Sound: The Falcon *zooms by.*

THREEPIO: <Ooss, nooch, Vader! Han Solo tee ka low carbon!>

Sound: Boom of the carbonite slab falling flat in the Cloud City facility.

THREEPIO: <Ee day kochna goobo sahnic. Oh . . .>

Sound: The sizzle and crash of a lightsaber duel. Meanwhile, a cub's purring begins. Closer to listeners' POV.

HAN: *(SOTTO VOCE)* Whoa, what gives? Why's this kid huggin' me?

LEIA: *(SOTTO VOCE)* Looks like you've got a fan.

HAN: Okay, short stuff, but quit teething on my finger.

THREEPIO: <Howoon, kee nee chatto toe mo mon efka.>

EWOKS: REACT TO THE LATEST REVELATION, CONFERRING AMONG THEMSELVES AND CHATTERING TO THEIR GUESTS.

LUKE: What're they saying, Threepio?

THREEPIO: The Ewoks want to know where they fit into the story, sir. They wish their deeds against the Empire to be remembered, too.

HAN: What?

THREEPIO: Myth and life are strongly intertwined for Ewoks. If I make them part of the tale, it will in their minds make them part of the Rebellion.

LUKE: Do it, Threepio. Defeating the Empire is their only hope, just as it's ours.

THREEPIO: Very good, Master Luke. *(GOES BACK TO HIS AUDIENCE)* <Latota sall qee Endor, nu Ewoks munturi.>

EWOKS: AN EVEN BIGGER "AHHH!," AND APPROBATION.

THREEPIO: <Jamoo fu Wicket chawa Logray. Koro Chief Chirpa pahchka.>

EWOKS: THEY LOVE IT.

THREEPIO: <Peech kama ee eekwi Death Star.>

Sound: Firing of snub fighters' laser cannons and the resulting explosion of the new Death Star.

EWOKS: EXULT, THEN FALL INTO "TOWN MEETING" DEBATE. REACHES A CRESCENDO, THEN FALLS AWAY. CHIEF CHIRPA MAKES A PROCLAMATION UNDER NEXT EXCHANGE.

HAN: *(NO LONGER SOTTO VOCE)* What's going on?

LEIA: I don't know.

THREEPIO: Wonderful!

LUKE: Threepio, translation please?

THREEPIO: Chief Chirpa says that we are now a part of the tribe.

HAN: Just what I always wanted.

LEIA: They could be important allies, Han. They've even got war machines—primitive, but they could be useful.

HAN: Oh, dandy. Maybe they've got a wooden turbo-laser cannon.

LUKE: Maybe they do. *(FALTERS DURING NEXT, SENSING VADER'S PRESENCE)* You have to look beyond appearances— ["—Han; they sometimes hide a greater truth."]

LEIA: Luke, what's wrong?

LUKE: Nothing, I'm okay. *(MOVING OFF)* I just need some air.

EWOKS: RAISING A CELEBRATORY RUCKUS.

Music: Ewok music strikes up. Tom-toms, "cow bells," etc.

HAN: LAUGHS. *(TO OFF)* Might as well give in, there, Chewie. They're not gonna leave you alone till you dance.

CHEWBACCA: GIVES A BEMUSED CATERWAUL.

HAN: Yeah, short help is better than no help at all, pal.

WICKET: CHATTERS TO HAN.

HAN: Um, thanks, Wicket. It's a real honor. Thank you.

THREEPIO: Wicket is saying the Ewok scouts are going to show us the quickest way to the Imperial shield generator.

HAN: Good. How far is it?

THREEPIO: Eh?

HAN: Go on, ask him.

THREEPIO: <Grau neeka—>

HAN: *(INTERRUPTING)* Wait, where'd Luke go? He's gotta hear this. Threepio, tell Wicket we need some fresh supplies, too.

THREEPIO: Ahem! <Chee oto pah—>

HAN: And Threepio, try to get our weapons back.

LEIA: *(MOVING OFF)* I'll go find Luke.

THREEPIO: <Umma freeda—>

HAN: And hurry up, will ya? I haven't got all day.

THREEPIO: Why, sir? Are there other droids you need to drive to distraction before retiring?

SCENE 5-5   EWOK VILLAGE EXTERIOR

Sound: The celebration is in the distance, night forest noises now heard in background. Leia's footsteps on the log walkway move on, under next.

LEIA: *(MOVING ON)* Luke? Luke, why did you leave the meeting? What's bothering you?

LUKE: Leia . . . do you remember your mother? Your real mother?

LEIA: Yeah, just a little. She died when I was very young.

LUKE: What do you remember?

LEIA: Just . . . images, really. Feelings.

LUKE: Tell me.

LEIA: She was very beautiful. Kind, but . . . sad. Why are you asking me this?

LUKE: I have no memory of my mother. I never knew her.

LEIA: What is it, Luke? What's troubling you?

LUKE: Vader is here. Now, on this moon.

LEIA: How do you know?

LUKE: I feel his presence. He's come for me. He can feel it when I'm near. As long as I stay here I'm endangering the group and our mission. I have to go. I have to face him.

LEIA: Why?

LUKE: Because he's my father.

LEIA: Your father?

LUKE: There's more. It won't be easy for you to hear this but you must. If I don't make it back, you're the only hope for the Alliance.

LEIA: Luke, don't talk that way. You have a power . . . I don't understand and I could never have.

LUKE: You're wrong, Leia. You have that power, too. In time you'll learn to use it as I have. The Force is strong in my family. My father has it. I have it. And my sister has it.

LEIA: Sister . . .

LUKE: Yes. It's you, Leia.

LEIA: I know. Somehow . . . I've always known.

LUKE: Then you know why I have to face him.

LEIA: No! Luke, run away. If he can feel your presence, then leave this place. I wish I could go with you.

LUKE: No you don't. You've always been strong. You were strong when you slew Jabba the Hutt to free yourself.

LEIA: Yes, I . . . I thought of the evil Jabba had done, and suddenly I was strong, stronger than I'd ever been. It frightened me later, the strength I had at that moment.

LUKE: You see? You're the daughter of Anakin Skywalker. Darth Vader.

LEIA: But why must you confront him?

LUKE: Because . . . there is still good in him. I've felt it. He won't turn me over to the Emperor. I can save him. I know I can. I can turn him back from the dark side of the Force. I have to do it, Leia.

LEIA: I think I knew that, too.

LUKE: I must leave now. *(MOVING OFF)* May the Force be with you, Leia.

LEIA: And with you . . . Luke . . .

Sound: Han's bootsteps moving on.

HAN: *(MOVING ON)* Luke? Leia? Hey, Leia! What's goin' on?

LEIA: Nothing, Han. I just want to be alone for a little bit.

HAN: Nothing? Come on, tell me. What's the problem?

LEIA: . . . I can't tell you.

HAN: Could you tell Luke? Is that who you could tell?

LEIA: Han, I—["—can't betray a secret, but it's not what you're thinking."]

HAN: *(MOVING PARTWAY OFF)* Ahh, forget I asked . . .

Sound: His bootsteps stop.

HAN: Naw, wait. That's not how I want to leave this. *(MOVING BACK ON)* I'm sorry, Leia.

LEIA: Just hold me, Han.

SCENE 5-6 INTERIOR, LANDING PLATFORM, IMPERIAL HQ ON ENDOR

Sound: Tech sounds, marching Imperials, the distant tread of AT-ATs and the hum of a shuttle lifting off.

IMPERIAL COMMANDER: Lord Vader, we've brought a Rebel who surrendered to us at the forest perimeter. He was armed only with this lightsaber.

Sound: Vader's respirator moves on.

VADER: I'll take it, Commander.

COMMANDER: The captive denies it, but I believe there may be more of them. I request permission to conduct a thorough search of the area.

VADER: Permission granted, Commander. Conduct your search and bring his companions to me.

COMMANDER: Yes, m'lord. *(MOVING OFF)*

Sound: Guard detail's footsteps move off.

VADER: The Emperor has been expecting you.

LUKE: I know, Father.

VADER: So, you have accepted the truth.

LUKE: I've accepted the truth that you were once Anakin Sky-walker—my father.

VADER: That name has no longer any meaning for me.

LUKE: It is the name of your true self. You've only forgotten. I know there is good in you. The Emperor hasn't driven it from you fully. That was why you couldn't destroy me. That's why you won't bring me to your Emperor now.

VADER: I see you have constructed a new lightsaber.

Sound: Vader fires up the sword, runs it through a flourish or two.

VADER: Your Jedi skills are complete.

Sound: Vader shuts the blade down.

VADER: Indeed you are powerful, as the Emperor has foreseen.

LUKE: Then come away with me, Father.

VADER: Obi-Wan once thought as you do. You don't know the power of the dark side. I must obey my master.

LUKE: I will not turn . . . and you'll be compelled to kill me.

VADER: If that is your destiny . . .

LUKE: Search your feelings, Father. You can't do this. I feel the conflict within you. Let go of your hate.

VADER: It is too late for me, Son. I have no choice but to bring you before the Emperor. He will show you the true nature of the Force. He is your master now.

SCENE 5-7 EXTERIOR ENDOR

Sound: Morning on the forest floor with attendant noises.

WICKET: CHATTERS EXCITEDLY BUT IN LOW TONE.

HAN: *(SOFTLY)* There's only a few guards. This shouldn't be too much trouble. Yeah, I see it. Keep your voice down, Wicket.

LEIA: *(SOFTLY)* The Ewoks were right. This back door to the bunker complex isn't nearly as well protected as the main entrance.

THREEPIO: *(SOFTLY)* They assure me that it does give access to the shield generator installation.

HAN: That's all we need. Wait, where'd our lookout go?

THREEPIO: I don't know, sir. Paploo appears to have slipped off on his own—what is it, Wicket?

WICKET: <Ah, ah! Gareeta! Koonta. E gu kimbu.>

HAN: Well, as long as he stays out of our way. You ready, Chewie?

CHEWBACCA: RUMBLES QUIETLY IN THE AFFIRMATIVE.

LEIA: Watch out for the guards to the left, by the speeder bikes. It only takes one to raise the alarm.

HAN: Then we'll take 'em out real quiet-like.

LEIA: Weren't you saying something like that only yesterday?

HAN: Cute. *(TO CHEWBACCA)* Okay, Chewie—["—you work your way around to their left flank and I'll come in from the right."]

THREEPIO: Oh my! Princess Leia, look there, beyond the speeder bikes.

HAN: Where—oh, man! Paploo!

THREEPIO: I'm afraid our furry little companion has gone and done something rather rash.

HAN: There goes our surprise attack.

THREEPIO: He's stealing a speeder. But—he can't possibly know how to fly one safely.

HAN: Safety ain't the point of a joyride, Threepio.

LEIA: There's the voice of experience.

Sound: Paploo kicks over the speeder's engine, off.

HAN: I don't believe it. He's got the engine fired up.

IMPERIAL SCOUT #1: *(OFF, VOICE PROCESSED TO INDICATE HELMET EXTERNAL SPEAKER)* Look! Over there! Stop him!

PAPLOO: DOES AN EWOK "HI-HO SILVER," OFF. HIS WAR CRY MOVES OFF, WITH NEXT.

Sound: The speeder bike belches power and moves off.

THREEPIO: There he goes! He's clinging on to the handlebars for dear life.

Sound: Three more air hogs crank up and vroom off in pursuit, under next.

HAN: It'll be interesting to hear how he got along without using the foot pedals.

LEIA: Brilliant! Don't you see what he's done? Diversionary tactics! Paploo's drawn away all the sentinels but one.

HAN: Not bad for a little furball. Get the commandos into position. *(MOVING OFF)* Chewie and me'll take care of the last guard.

CHEWBACCA: *(MOVING OFF)* A GUTTURAL EAGERNESS.

LEIA: *(MOVING OFF)* Threepio, keep out of the line of fire.

WICKET: NATTERS AND COMMENTS.

THREEPIO: "Line of fire?" Artoo, Wicket, I have decided we shall remain right here.

ARTOO: RASPBERRIES THE NOTION OF MISSING OUT ON THE ACTION.

SCENE 5-8   BACK AT THE BUNKER ENTRANCE

Sound: Transition from forest woodline to bunker clearing.

SCOUT #2: *(TO COMLINK, VOICE PROCESSED TO SIGNIFY HEL-MET)* Headquarters, any word yet on pursuit—["—of that runaway perpetrator who hijacked a speeder bike at this location?"]

Sound: Han's finger tapping the scout's armored shoulder.

HAN: Excuse me, pal. Is this where I sign up for the bunker tour?

SCOUT #2: *(REACTS)* What? Who—Halt! Get your hands up!

HAN: *(MOVING PARTWAY OFF, LEADING THE IMPERIAL ON)* No, I don't think so . . .

SCOUT #2: *(INDICATING EFFORT OF GIVING BRIEF CHASE, THEN SKIDDING TO A STOP AS HE REALIZES HE'S BEEN AM-BUSHED)* I said halt! Stop where you are—["—and place your hands behind your head, interlocking your fingers."]

LEIA: Freeze! Drop that weapon, Private.

CHEWBACCA: ADDS HIS OWN THREAT.

SCOUT #2: Rebels!

HAN: He's all yours, Major Derlin.

MAJOR DERLIN: Yes, sir. *(TO HIS TROOPS)* Keep the prisoner covered. You two, disarm him.

Sound: Rattle of scout's blaster being taken, under next.

LEIA: The complex door's unlocked, Han.

HAN: Okay, Major. Let's go.

DERLIN: Right.

Sound: Derlin's comlink tones as he opens a channel, under next.

DERLIN: *(TO COMLINK)* Demolition squad, prepare to move out. I want two fire teams to establish security at this point. Gimme a three-hundred-sixty-degree field of fire, centered on this airlock door.

SCENE 5-9 EMPEROR'S THRONE ROOM ON THE DEATH STAR

Sound: Throne room door opens and Vader's respirator moves on, as do his and Luke's bootsteps, under next.

VADER: *(MOVING ON)* I have brought our new slave as you commanded, my master.

EMPEROR: Ahhh . . .

LUKE: Your prisoner but not your slave, Palpatine.

EMPEROR: Welcome to my new Death Star, young Skywalker. I have been expecting you.

VADER: What is thy bidding, my master?

EMPEROR: We've no further need to keep our guest's wrists shackled, do we? Would you not prefer it if your binders opened of their own accord, young man?

Sound: The binder gyves' lock mechanism activates in response to the Emperor's will, releasing. The binders snick open and clatter to the floor with a metallic din.

LUKE: Such a minor feat, for the Emperor of the galaxy.

EMPEROR: I look forward to completing your training. In time you, too, will call me "Master."

LUKE: You're gravely mistaken. You won't convert me as you did my father.

EMPEROR: Oh, no, my young Jedi. You will find that it is you who are mistaken . . . about a great many things.

VADER: Here is his lightsaber, my master.

EMPEROR: Ah, yes, a Jedi's weapon. Very much like Anakin Skywalker's. By now you must know your father can never be turned from the dark side. So it will be with you.

LUKE: You're wrong. Soon I'll be dead . . . and you with me.

EMPEROR: *(LAUGHS)* Perhaps you refer to the imminent attack of your Rebel fleet.

LUKE: I . . .

EMPEROR: Yes . . . I assure you that we here in the Death Star are quite safe from your friends.

LUKE: Your overconfidence is your weakness.

EMPEROR: Your naive faith in your friends is yours.

VADER: It is pointless to resist, my son.

EMPEROR: Everything that has transpired has done so according to my design. Your friends down there on the Sanctuary Moon of Endor are walking into a trap. As is your scruffy little armada. It was I who permitted the Alliance to discover the location of the defensive shield generator.

LUKE: You're bluffing.

EMPEROR: No, our bunker complex is quite safe from your pitiful band of commandos. A legion of my best troops awaits them in ambush.

LUKE: I don't believe you.

EMPEROR: But you will. Yes, I'm afraid the deflector shield of this battle station will be fully operational when your fleet arrives. We will entrap your friends in a killing box, and grind them up within it. And so will end, forever, the Rebel Alliance.

Sound: Scene fades.

NARRATOR: Emperor Palpatine has ensnared his prey at the very moment when patterns of the Force are converging. All unaware, the friends who matter most to Luke Skywalker tread on the brink of the abyss. And it seems that in the battlefield of Darth Vader's heart, Luke has already met defeat. But not all is yet said. Not all is done. The Jedi fire still flickers in the universe, in one last, lone Knight. That flame must now shine forth at its brightest, or go dark forever.

Music: Closing theme up under credits.

NARRATOR: CLOSING CREDITS.

EPISODE SIX:

"BLOOD OF A JEDI"

CAST:
Han
Leia
Major Derlin
Threepio
Lando
Wedge
Gray Leader
Green Leader
Admiral Ackbar
Red Two
Red Three
Luke
Emperor Palpatine
Darth Vader
Bunker Commander
Trooper #1
Control Room Voice
Anakin Skywalker (Unmasked Vader)

SOUND/FX ROLES:
Chewbacca
Artoo-Detoo
Wicket
Glider Ewok
Nien Nunb

ANNOUNCER: OPENING CREDITS.

Music: Opening theme.

NARRATOR: A long time ago in a galaxy far, far away there came a time of revolution, when Rebels united to challenge a tyrannical Empire. Now the endgame in this cosmic struggle has come. A combined Rebel fleet is on its way to the forest moon of the planet Endor, to destroy the Empire's new Death Star. But the Rebels are flying into a trap. Aboard the battle station, Luke Skywalker has fallen captive to Darth Vader. Luke's desperate appeals to turn him from the dark side of the Force have failed to move the man who was once Anakin Skywalker, his father. Below, on the lush green Sanctuary Moon, a Rebel commando unit has penetrated the underground complex from which the Death Star's defensive shield is generated. But the Rebels do not realize that their presence there is also a part of the grand strategy, hatched by their deadliest enemy, Emperor Palpatine.

SCENE 6-1   INTERIOR, ENDOR SHIELD GENERATOR BUNKER

Sound: Tech sounds, incidental noises of Imperial staff going about duties, etc., wild lines. Sound of a blaster bolt exploding the chamber door lock—Han Solo shooting his way in.

IMPERIALS: OUTCRIES, EXCLAMATIONS, WILD LINES.

Sound: Door sighs open, Han's and other Rebels' footsteps move on quickly.

HAN: *(MOVING ON)* Freeze! Everybody, hands in the air!

LEIA: *(MOVING ON)* Get your hands away from those controls!

REBEL COMMANDOS: *(MOVING ON)* WILD LINES, ORDERING IMPERIALS TO SURRENDER, ETC.

HAN: *(TO CHEWBACCA)* Chewie, cover those two in the corner.

CHEWBACCA: WOOFS A RESPONSE.

LEIA: Han, the fleet will be here any minute.

HAN: Major Derlin?

DERLIN: Yes, right here, General.

HAN: The clock's running out, Major. Let's do it.

DERLIN: *(TO HIS TROOPS)* Demolition squad up! Start planting your charges. Security teams, disarm the prisoners and get them up against that far wall.

REBELS: WILD LINES AND HUBBUB AS THEY CARRY OUT ORDERS.

IMPERIALS: REACT TO REBELS, ETC.

Sound: Chunk and thud as demolition charges are planted. They click and ping as they're activated. Imperial weapons being piled on the floor.

HAN: What happened to the droids and the Ewoks? Didn't they follow us in?

LEIA: I guess they stayed back at the edge of the forest. Han, if this shield isn't down when Lando and the others emerge from hyperspace, they'll be like targets in a shooting gallery.

HAN: Relax, we're gonna blow this place clear over the Death Star. *(TO OFF)* Throw me another demo charge! Come on, come on!

SCENE 6-2   ENDOR FOREST NEAR BUNKER

Sound: Woodland noises. Wicket's chatter and Artoo's S/FX.

THREEPIO: Oh, I do hope the princess and General Solo hurry, Artoo.

ARTOO: WARBLES A QUESTION.

THREEPIO: No, I have no idea where the other Ewoks have gone. I'll ask Wicket—

WICKET: CHATTERS EXCITEDLY.

THREEPIO: Wicket, calm yourself.

WICKET: HIGHLY AGITATED.

THREEPIO: Stormtroopers? Where—oh—Imperial scout walkers!

Sound: Imperial troops and two-legged "scout walker" AT-ST, off.

THREEPIO: This is an ambush! The princess and the others will be captured. And the Rebel Fleet is already on its way—oh, this is a catastrophe!

WICKET: MUMBLES AND RUMBLES, MOVING OFF WITH PURPOSE.

THREEPIO: Wicket, you can't abandon us! You said the Ewoks would be loyal to the Rebel Alliance.

ARTOO: BURBLES A DETERMINED SIGNAL, MOVING OFF.

THREEPIO: Artoo, where are you going? *(MOVING OFF)* Wait, come back! Artoo, stay with me.

SCENE 6-3 *FALCON* COCKPIT

Sound: Endor fades. Transition to the cockpit of the Millennium Falcon. *Engines have the labored sound indicating emergence from hyperspace.*

LANDO: *(TO COMMO)* Assault Wing, this is Gold Leader. Prepare for emergence from hyperspace . . . now.

Sound: The big wind-down, as the ship goes subluminal.

LANDO: There's the Death Star, right on the mark. Nien Nunb, take the controls while I form up the wing.

NIEN NUNB: <Un-gate-oh.>

Sound: Controls and instruments, as Lando's Sullustan co-pilot conns the ship.

LANDO: Assault Wing, all flight leaders report in.

WEDGE: *(OVER COMMO)* Red Leader standing by.

GRAY LEADER: *(OVER COMMO)* Gray Leader standing by.

GREEN LEADER: *(OVER COMMO)* Green Leader standing by.

WEDGE: Lock all S-foils in attack position.

ACKBAR: *(OVER COMMO)* This is Admiral Ackbar. Commence your approach on the Death Star. And may the Force be with us.

LANDO: Assault Wing, form up on me.

NIEN NUNB: <Ah-teh-yairee u-hareh mu-ah-hareh.>

LANDO: What? Try again, Nien. We've got to get some kind of reading on that deflector shield, up or down.

NIEN NUNB: <Mu-ah-hareh mu-kay, huh?>

LANDO: Well how could the Imperials be jamming us if they don't know . . . we're coming . . . ?

NIEN NUNB: <E-mutee bit-chu me.>

LANDO: *(TO COMMO)* Assault Wing, break off the attack! The Death Star shield is still up.

Sound: Cockpit alarms, sensor warning indicators. Falcon *labors as she goes into evasive maneuvers. Add sounds of snub fighters doing same.*

WEDGE: *(OVER COMMO)* I get no reading, boss. Are you sure?

LANDO: All craft, pull up and regroup.

ACKBAR: *(OVER COMMO)* This is Ackbar. It's a trap! All vessels take evasive action. Green Flight, stick close to holding sector MV-seven.

Sound: A new cockpit alarm comes up, under next.

WEDGE: *(OVER COMMO)* Admiral, we have enemy ships in sector forty-seven.

LANDO: Admiral, we've got TIE fighters coming in.

GRAY LEADER: *(OVER COMMO)* They're all over the place. They're boxing us in.

LANDO: Accelerate to attack speed. Draw them away from the cruisers.

WEDGE: Copy, Gold Leader.

Sound: Falcon *and snubs engage the TIE fighters.*

LANDO: Watch yourself, Wedge. Three of 'em coming in high on your six.

WEDGE: Red Three, Red Two, close up.

RED TWO: We're on 'em.

RED THREE: Three eyeballs, twenty degrees high.

WEDGE: Scissor left. I'll take the leader.

Sound: More dogfighting.

ACKBAR: Green Flight, stand by to provide cover while we pull the cruisers back.

WEDGE: I nailed the leader but the rest are headed for the medical frigate.

LANDO: I'm on my way, Wedge.

NIEN NUNB: <Lamou-be-o-tee.>

LANDO: Yeah. I see it.. Only the TIE fighters are attacking. I wonder what those Star Destroyers are waiting for?

WEDGE: Boss, something's happening over on that Death Star.

LANDO: Forget it for now. We can't get at it through that deflector shield and it can't hurt us.

RED TWO: Heads up, heads up. Death Star is firing!

Sound: The Death Star fires its planet-killer weapon, followed by a tremendous explosion.

LANDO: The Death Star took out one of the cruisers! That thing is operational! *(TO COMMO) Home One*, this is Gold Leader.

ACKBAR: We saw it, Gold Leader. All craft regroup for a general withdrawal.

LANDO: We won't get another chance at that battle station, Admiral.

ACKBAR: We have no choice, General Calrissian. Our cruisers can't repel firepower of that magnitude.

LANDO: Han will have that deflector shield down. We've got to give him more time.

ACKBAR: Time is something we don't have much of, Gold Leader.

SCENE 6-4   EMPEROR'S THRONE ROOM, DEATH STAR

Sound: The space battle intensifies, then fades. Emperor's throne room on Death Star comes up, with Vader's breathing in the background.

EMPEROR: *(TO LUKE, SLIGHTLY OFF)* Come and see, young Sky-walker. From here on the Death Star we shall have an excellent view of the battle.

LUKE: You're not going to win, Emperor Palpatine.

EMPEROR: Oh no? Your Rebel fleet has discovered my trap, but not soon enough to save itself from annihilation. Such a pity. Come to the observation port and see for yourself.

LUKE: You think it is your powers that have brought us to this moment. You are mistaken. It is the Force.

EMPEROR: Indeed. The dark side. Isn't that so, Lord Vader?

VADER: As you say, my master.

EMPEROR: From here, boy, you will witness the final destruction of the Alliance, and the end of your insignificant Rebellion.

LUKE: No. It won't. It can't end like this.

EMPEROR: Ah, I see you looking to your lightsaber. You want it, don't you? The hate is swelling in you now. Well? Here it lies, next to my hand. Take your Jedi weapon.

LUKE: That would be your final triumph, wouldn't it?

VADER: The dark side is the ultimate power, Luke.

EMPEROR: Look out there! Your comrades are being exterminated. Use your lightsaber, young Jedi. I am unarmed. Strike me down with it. Give in to your anger.

LUKE: No!

EMPEROR: It is unavoidable. It is your destiny, young Skywalker. You, like your father, are now mine!

SCENE 6-5 EXTERIOR ENDOR BUNKER

Sound: Heavy servo and grinding indicates opening of the blast door. Sound of Rebels' steps and stormtroopers armored ones moving on.

BUNKER COMMANDER: *(MOVING ON)* Keep moving, you Rebel trash! You there, keep your hands behind your head.

LEIA: *(MOVING ON)* Get your hands off me.

HAN: *(MOVING ON)* Leia, stay close to me.

BUNKER COMMANDER: *(TO LINE OF POWs)* Rebel prisoners, halt! Stay in line and keep your hands raised.

LEIA: Han, we've got to do something.

HAN: Yeah, well, a battalion of Imperial scout walkers could make that a problem.

Sound: A two-legged scout walker strides by, off.

HAN: Chewie, you okay?

CHEWBACCA: SNARLS THAT HE IS.

HAN: Good. Stay ready.

LEIA: Han, Lando and the fleet are finished if we don't neutralize that shield generator.

HAN: We're not going to be helping 'em if we get ourselves mowed down by ["—the Imperials. We have to wait for a chance to turn the tables."]

BUNKER COMMANDER: Attention, prisoners! You are going to be transported—["—to the headquarters platform for interrogation and processing."]

THREEPIO: *(FROM OFF)* Hello! I say you over there!

LEIA: Threepio and Artoo.

THREEPIO: Were you looking for me?

ARTOO: DOES A QUICK HAILING SIGNAL, OFF.

BUNKER COMMANDER: Where did those droids come from? Get over there and take them into custody.

LEIA: What's going on?

HAN: I dunno. Get set for anything.

161

Sound: Troopers hurrying over to nab the droids. Wild lines over helmet comlinks as they double time to obey, moving off.

TROOPER: You two grab those droids on the hill.

THREEPIO: There's no need for violence. As a matter of fact, there are some local denizens eager to make your acquaintance.

Sound: An Ewok hunting/war horn is blown, off. Sounds of the attacking teddy bears leaping down out of the branches.

EWOKS: WILD BATTLE CRIES, ETC.

LEIA: It's the Ewoks! They're springing an ambush.

BUNKER COMMANDER: *(MOVING OFF)* You men there, form a firing line!

TROOPER: *(OFF)* We can't, sir. Our men are in the line of fire.

HAN: Chewie, take out the guards! *(INDICATES ACT OF SWINGING ONE STORMTROOPER INTO ANOTHER)*

CHEWBACCA: ACKNOWLEDGES.

Sound: Armored troopers slammed together.

TROOPERS: REACT AS THEY'RE DOWNED.

Sound: Release of catapult, flights of Ewok arrows. Spasmodic shots from the troopers.

LEIA: Watch out. Those arrows aren't choosy who they hit.

HAN: Leia! Grab a blaster!

Sound: Han firing his blaster.

HAN: Gotta get back inside that bunker.

Sound: Heavy twang of a catapult releasing, off. Impact of boulders hitting a scout walker, bonking off the armor.

LEIA: The Ewoks are throwing boulders with catapults!

HAN: Either that or they've got some mighty slow meteors around here. Try the bunker door.

LEIA: Got it!

HAN: I'll see if I can spot Derlin.

Sound: Leia manipulates the lock touchpad, but elicits only "invalid"/"access denied" buzzes, etc., under next.

LEIA: The access code's been changed. We need Artoo-Detoo.

HAN: Try the comlink.

Sound: Leia punches up a call on the comlink.

LEIA: *(TO COMLINK)* Artoo, where are you? We need you and Threepio at the bunker door right away.

ARTOO: *(VIA COMLINK)* RESPONDS WITH A RESOLUTE SERIES OF TONES.

HAN: The strike team's pinned down. Looks like it's up to us.

SCENE 6-6 *FALCON* COCKPIT

Sound: Cockpit comes up, the starship still dogfighting, evading enemy fire, etc.

WEDGE: *(OVER COMLINK)* Gold Leader, this is Red Leader. Repeat your last message.

LANDO: *(TO COMLINK)* I said closer, Wedge! Move as close as you can to those Star Destroyers and engage them at point-blank range.

ACKBAR: *(OVER COMLINK)* At that distance we won't last long against those Dreadnaughts.

LANDO: *(TO COMLINK)* We'll last longer than we would against that Death Star. And we might just take a few of them with us.

LANDO: All flights, regroup! Close it up and stick with your wing-men. *(TO HIMSELF)* Come on, Han, old buddy. Don't let me down.

Sound: Falcon fades.

SCENE 6-7   EMPEROR'S THRONE ROOM

Sound: Emperor's throne room comes up again. Vader's breathing in background.

EMPEROR: You see, young Skywalker? Your fleet is lost. Your companions on the Sanctuary Moon will not survive. There is no escape, my young apprentice.

LUKE: The battle's not over yet.

EMPEROR: Ah, good. I can feel your anger. I am defenseless. Here, take up your lightsaber. Strike me down with all your hatred . . .

LUKE: No . . .

VADER: The hour has come for you to join us, Luke.

LUKE: No . . .

EMPEROR: Then you must watch your friends perish!

LUKE: No! *(INDICATES EFFORT OF SNATCHING UP THE LIGHTSABER)*

Sound: Rattle and whoosh of the weapon as Luke summons it to him off the throne arm, followed by the signature sound of the lightsaber firing up, under next.

EMPEROR: So, the Jedi summons his lightsaber and it flies to his hand.

LUKE: I won't let you kill them.

VADER: Yes! You will!

Sound: Vader's lightsaber enkindles, spitting and humming.

VADER: It's beyond your control now, Luke.

Sound: The two blades crackle and hiss, as Vader knocks Luke's aside.

LUKE: REACTS TO BEING PUSHED BACK.

LUKE: I have to stop him.

VADER: You will fail.

LUKE: INDICATES EFFORT OF HIS ATTACK.

Sound: The deflagrating blades clash and sizzle again as the battle is joined. Various furnishings, structural members, etc., are cleaved or set aflame, under next.

LUKE: INDICTATES EXCHANGES OF SWORD STROKES, ETC., UNDER NEXT.

VADER: THE SAME.

EMPEROR: *(LAUGHS IN DELIGHT)* That's it! Glorious! Use your aggressive feelings, boy! Let the hate flow through you.

LUKE: *(BACKING OFF, PANTING)* No. This is wrong.

Sound: Luke flicks off his lightsaber.

LUKE: I won't do it.

VADER: Obi-Wan has taught you well.

LUKE: I will not fight you, Father.

VADER: You are unwise to lower your defenses . . .

Sound: Vader's blade swishes and moans as he takes another cut at Luke.

LUKE: INDICATES EFFORT AS HE JUMPS CLEAR. [NOTE: A RE-VERSE FLIP TO A CATWALK, IN THE FILM.]

Sound: Luke lands on the catwalk, above the others' heads.

EMPEROR: *(LAUGHS)* Dodge and leap, foolish boy. There isn't enough room in the galaxy for you to avoid your fate.

LUKE: Your thoughts betray you, Father. I feel the good in you . . . the conflict.

VADER: There is no conflict. Come down from the catwalk.

LUKE: You couldn't bring yourself to kill me before and I don't believe you'll destroy me now.

EMPEROR: Cut the catwalk out from under him, Vader. I would see the last of the Jedi brought low.

VADER: You underestimate the power of the dark side, Luke. If you will not fight, then you will meet your destiny.

LUKE: You don't mean that, Father.

VADER: I mean this. *(INDICATES EFFORT OF TAKING THE CAT-WALK SUPPORTS OUT WITH ONE SLASH)* [NOTE: IN THE FILM, VADER THROWS HIS LIGHTSABER TO ACCOMPLISH THIS.]

Sound: Catwalk is undercut as metal slags and girders part. It comes crashing down to the throne room floor with a metallic din.

LUKE: REACTS TO FALL.

VADER: Yield to the dark side, Luke.

LUKE: Never. *(EXERTS HIMSELF TO WIN FREE OF THE DEBRIS AND ESCAPE VADER'S FOLLOW-UP ATTACK)*

Sound: Wreckage shifting and clanging as Luke extricates himself and escapes.

EMPEROR: Go after him, Vader. Bring him to ground.

VADER: *(MOVING OFF)* I will bring him to you, my master.

Sound: Vader's breathing and bootsteps move off. Then throne room fades.

SCENE 6-8   ENDOR EXTERIOR

Sound: Bunker clearing on Endor comes up, with Ewok-stormtrooper battle still raging in background.

LEIA: Hurry, Artoo! Get that blast door open!

ARTOO: TWEEDLES HIS DETERMINATION.

Sound: Instrumentation noises, as the astro-droid works to hack the door lock mechanism.

HAN: Now or never, Artoo.

THREEPIO: Please permit my counterpart to concentrate— ["—General Solo."]

LEIA: Heads up! Stormtrooper!

Sound: Incoming round hits Artoo, knocking him away from the door terminal, frying his circuits.

ARTOO: YELLS IN FRIGHT AND AGONY.

LEIA: Artoo!

HAN: *(TO TROOPER, OFF)* Lousy backshooter!

Sound: Han fires his blaster. Shot hits armored Imperial, off.

TROOPER: MOANS, FALLING, OFF.

THREEPIO: Artoo, you've been shot!

ARTOO: A WEAK "THEY GOT ME" WHEEZE.

THREEPIO: My goodness! Artoo, why did you have to be so brave?

HAN: I suppose I could apply a little Corellian Overdrive—hot-wire the door.

LEIA: I'll cover you.

Sound: Han begins hacking the door terminal controls.

LEIA: How can those Ewoks hold their own against the Imperials?

HAN: *(DISTRACTEDLY)* It's their turf and their ambush. Makes all the difference.

LEIA: C'mon, Han, we're running out of time.

HAN: I think I've got it. Here goes. *(INDICATES THROWING THE ACTIVATOR SWITCH)*

Sound: The switch clicks, followed by activation tones. Immediately, heavy motors pound and the door channels grind as a second portal slides into place over the first, under next.

THREEPIO: Wait! You've locked the outer shield into place over the blast door!

HAN: Crummy Imperial equipment.

Sound: Another incoming blaster round, this one striking close and grazing Leia.

LEIA: CRIES OUT AS SHE'S WOUNDED.

THREEPIO: Oh my stars, Princess Leia! She's been shot!

HAN: *(INDICATES HOLDING HER CLOSE, CHECKING HER WOUND)* Leia, where'd they get you?

LEIA: *(IN PAIN)* Shoulder . . .

TROOPER #1: *(FROM OFF, VOICE OVER HELMET SPEAKER)* Freeze, Rebels!

THREEPIO: Oh dear!

TROOPER #1: *(OFF)* Nobody move.

HAN: *(SOTTO VOCE, TO LEIA)* I guess they've got us.

LEIA: *(SOTTO VOCE, TO HAN)* I've still got my blaster. When I give the word, get out of my way fast.

HAN: I love you.

LEIA: I know.

TROOPER #1: *(FROM OFF)* Get on your feet!

HAN: You heard the man.

LEIA: Ready . . . now! *(INDICATES EFFORT OF BRINGING THE GUN UP FOR SNAP SHOTS)*

HAN: INDICATES GETTING OUT OF HER LINE OF FIRE.

Sound: Leia fires twice.

TROOPER #1: YELLS OUT, SHOT.

HAN: Nice play, Princess.

LEIA: Just a little Corellian Overdrive.

THREEPIO: Look out! There's a scout walker closing in on us.

Sound: A scout-walker AT-ST comes clomping on, sounding like a biped M-1 tank. It creaks to a stop, under next.

HAN: *(TO THE WALKER)* Don't shoot! We give up!

Sound: The AT-ST walker chugs to a halt. Topside hatch unlatches, hinges creak, and it falls open with a clang, under next.

LEIA: It stopped.

THREEPIO: General Solo, I never knew you could be so persuasive.

LEIA: They're opening the top turret.

CHEWBACCA: MOANS.

HAN: Chewie! Look, it's Chewie!

CHEWBACCA: A HAPPY GREETING, FROM OFF.

THREEPIO: He's captured a scout walker.

HAN: *(TO CHEWIE, OFF)* Chewie, get down here—no. Wait. I'm coming up there; I've got an idea. Cover the bunker door with your guns.

CHEWBACCA: ROOOFS AN AFFIRMATIVE, OFF.

Sound: Scout walker cranks up and reshuffles a few steps, under next.

LEIA: Looks like Major Derlin and the Ewoks are coming to help.

HAN: Fine, they can help us throw a little surprise party.

SCENE 6-9   INTERIOR SCOUT WALKER COCKPIT/ EXTERIOR BUNKER DOOR

Sound: Short transition to denote brief passage of time.

HAN: Scout Walker Seven to shield control room, come in.

CONTROL ROOM VOICE: *(VIA COMLINK)* This is the shield control room. What is your status out there?

HAN: Battle's over out here, Commander. The Rebels are fleeing into the woods. But we need reinforcements.

CONTROL: Outstanding! I'll send three squads. Unsealing the blast door now.

Sound: The outer shield and heavy blast door churn and squeal open, under next.

HAN: That's very, very accommodating of you, Commander.

CONTROL: This is a day that will long be remembered.

Sound: Comlink clicks off.

HAN: (ASIDE, TO PRINCESS) Ya got that right, pal.

IMPERIAL REINFORCEMENTS: COME CROWDING OUT THE BUNKER DOOR WITH SUITABLE WILD LINES, ETC., MOVING ON. THEY STUMBLE TO A HALT AS THEY REALIZE THEY'VE BEEN TAKEN PRISONER.

HAN: Hold it! Nobody move!

LEIA: Drop your weapons and place your hands above your heads!

HAN: Let's move it!

IMPERIAL REINFORCEMENTS: COWED AND GRUMBLING, THEY MOVE OFF.

LEIA: Major Derlin, did you recover any demolitions charges?

DERLIN: Plenty.

HAN: Get your teams busy.

DERLIN: (MOVING OFF) We're on it, General.

LEIA: The Rebel Fleet must be on the ropes by now.

HAN: Yeah, but in about sixty seconds the real party's gonna start.

THREEPIO: And we've still had no word of Master Luke.

SCENE 6-10   A DARK CORNER OF THE DEATH STAR THRONE ROOM

Sound: Vader's breathing sounding and his bootsteps echoing, off, as he stalks Luke.

VADER: Show yourself, Luke. A Jedi does not skulk in shadowy corners.

LUKE: I will not fight you.

VADER: Give yourself to the dark side. It is the only way you can save your friends.

LUKE: *(SOTTO VOCE, TO HIMSELF)* Never . . .

VADER: Yes. Your thoughts betray you. Your feelings for them are strong. Especially for . . .

Sound: The bootsteps stop and for a moment only Vader's respirator is heard.

VADER: . . . for your sister! So, you have a twin sister.

LUKE: *(SOTTO VOCE, TO HIMSELF)* Stop . . .

VADER: Your feelings have now betrayed her, too. Obi-Wan was wise to hide her from me.

LUKE: *(SOTTO VOCE, TO HIMSELF)* Go away . . .

VADER: Now his failure is complete. If you will not turn to the dark side, then perhaps your sister will.

LUKE: No!

Sound: Luke fires up his lightsaber.

LUKE: *(INDICATING THAT HE IS RUSHING TO THE ATTACK)* Leave her alone!

Sound: This time the blades join in exchanges of furious speed and violence. Collateral damage is done to columns and other objects around them as the two duel at unrelenting pace, under next.

EMPEROR: *(OFF)* That's it. *(LAUGHS)* Give way to the power of the dark side!

LUKE: I won't . . . let . . . you . . . hurt . . . her!

VADER: You cannot stop me.

LUKE: *(INDICATES EFFORT OF EACH STROKE, BUILDING TO THE FINAL, DECISIVE ONE)* I must . . . stop . . . you . . . Father!

Sound: Luke's last stroke takes Vader's right hand off, a coruscating explosion. Vader's lightsaber goes flying off, or deactivates.

VADER: ROARS IN RAGE LIKE A MORTALLY WOUNDED LION.

EMPEROR: Splendid! The son has struck off the father's hand, even as the father struck off the son's! *(LAUGHS)* Your hate has made you powerful, young Skywalker. Now: Fulfill your destiny and take your father's place at my side. Finish him!

LUKE: *(PANTING, SHAKING OFF HIS BERSERKERGANG)* I told you . . . no.

VADER: *(GASPING IN PAIN)* Why don't you . . . strike, Luke . . . ?

EMPEROR: Slay him, or I'll slay you.

LUKE: I'll never turn to the dark side.

Sound: Luke's lightsaber flicks off, goes silent. It clatters as he casts it aside.

LUKE: You've failed, Palpatine. I am a Jedi, like my father before me.

EMPEROR: And the last of them. So be it . . . Jedi. You are at the threshold of your ultimate defeat.

SCENE 6-11 *FALCON* COCKPIT

Sound: The ship's juking and firing in the ferocious space battle over Endor.

ACKBAR: *(OVER COMMO)* Gold Leader, the Death Star shield is down. Commence your attack on their main reactor.

LANDO: *(TO COMMO)* I told you Han and the others wouldn't let us down. *(TO NIEN NUNB)* Nien, retarget gunnery computers.

NIEN NUNB: <Deh-te'ill dou.>

LANDO: *(STILL TO COMMO, BUT NOW ADDRESSING HIS AS-SAULT WING)* Red Group, Gold Group—all remaining fighters, form up on me. We're going in.

WEDGE: *(OVER COMMO)* We copy, Gold Leader.

Sound: Falcon and snub fighters speeding to the attack.

WEDGE: There's the access tunnel coming up, boss.

LANDO: Tighten up your formation. We're flying straight to the heart of the Death Star.

RED TWO: *(OVER COMMO)* We've got TIE fighters on an inter-cept vector, boss.

LANDO: Keep 'em off our backs, but do not stop to engage. We have to hit that reactor.

WEDGE: Going in, Gold Leader.

Sound: Rebel ships zoom into the huge structural tunnel in the Death Star.

WEDGE: Tight quarters in here, boss.

LANDO: *(TO COMMO)* We're just here for a short visit. *(TO NIEN NUNB)* Nien, lock onto the strongest power source you can find. It should be the reactor.

NIEN NUNB: <Ah! Behb-e-twee muni.>

Sound: Controls and switches, indicators toning.

LANDO: Good. Keep us on that signal. Time to roll the dice.

SCENE 6-12   THRONE ROOM

Sound: Vader's labored, irregular breathing, in the background. There's a deep vibration, from the first explosions in the faraway reactor.

LUKE: The Death Star is doomed, Palpatine, and so is your Empire.

EMPEROR: Since you will not be turned, young Skywalker, you will be destroyed . . .

Sound: Crackling discharges of pure Force energy, as the Emperor summons up his power.

EMPEROR: Behold, the naked energies of the dark side. The lightning of pure willpower. Now feel its fury!

Sound: The dark side lightning bolts crash at Luke.

LUKE: CRIES OUT IN PAIN AND DISMAY.

EMPEROR: Young fool. Only now, at the end, do you understand.

Sound: Another megavolt volley from the Emperor.

LUKE: REACTS, NOW WEAKENED AND OVERWHELMED.

EMPEROR: Lord Vader, get to your feet. Rise, I say.

Sound: Vader's breathing irregular, shallow, denoting pain and injury.

VADER: *(INDICATING EFFORT OF DRAGGING HIMSELF TO HIS FEET)* Yes, my master.

EMPEROR: When I've slain this last Jedi, cast his body down the core shaft.

LUKE: No . . .

EMPEROR: Yes. Your feeble skills are no match for the power of the dark side. You now pay the price for your lack of vision. *(LAUGHS)*

Sound: Another bolt.

EMPEROR: I am beyond lightsabers. I am beyond Jedi ways. I am the dark side itself!

Sound: Yet another thunderbolt goes crashing. Luke slumps to the floor, under next.

LUKE: *(REACTS TO IMPACT) (TO VADER)* Father, please. Help me.

EMPEROR: He is my slave, not your father. Now, young Skywalker . . . you will die.

LUKE: Father . . .

Sound: Another dark side blast.

EMPEROR: Die!

LUKE: No . . .

EMPEROR: Yes!

VADER: *(INDICATING EFFORT OF SEIZING THE EMPEROR)* My son!

EMPEROR: Release me. Vader, I command you! *(REACTS TO BEING RAISED BODILY OVER VADER'S HEAD)* Put me down!

Sound: More crackling as Emperor's bolts crash.

VADER: *(GRIEVOUSLY INJURED)* I will: down the core shaft. Down to your death.

EMPEROR: Vader, I am your master!

VADER: Darth Vader's Master. But not Anakin Skywalker's! *(INDICATES EFFORT OF HURLING THE EMPEROR INTO THE SHAFT)*

EMPEROR: SHRIEKS IN TERROR, HIS VOICE TRAILING AWAY, AS HE PLUNGES TO HIS DEATH.

Sound: The Emperor's energy discharges trail off along with him. Those fade, and distant booming of final explosions.

LUKE: Father . . . Father . . .

VADER: It's over, Luke. *(INDICATES SUCCUMBING TO THE EFFECTS OF HIS WOUNDS AS HE TOPPLES)*

SCENE 6-13 *FALCON* COCKPIT

Sound: Falcon comes up with TIE fighter shooting, over commo.

RED THREE: Gold Leader, those TIEs are still with us.

LANDO: Red Two, peel off and take the rest of the Assault Wing back to the surface. Try to get those TIE fighters, or make them follow you out.

RED TWO: Copy, Gold Leader.

LANDO: Wedge, you stick with me.

WEDGE: I read you, boss.

NIEN NUNB: <Mu-kay.>

LANDO: I see it, I see it . . .

Sound: Falcon *clips a structural member for a grazing impact.*

LANDO: Whoops. There goes the paint job.

WEDGE: Reactor chamber coming up.

LANDO: Nien, prepare to fire.

NIEN NUNB: <Mu-teh gate-oh.>

Sound: More high-speed maneuvering as they enter the central reactor chamber.

WEDGE: There's the reactor, boss.

LANDO: You go for the power regulator on the north tower, Wedge. I'll target the central matrix.

WEDGE: Copy, Gold Leader.

LANDO: As an old pal of mine would say, "Let's blow this thing and go home." Steady . . .

LANDO: Fire!

Sound: Falcon*'s quad batteries pound the reactor matrix.*

WEDGE: Confirmed hits on both targets, boss.

LANDO: Now get clear. Go! Go!

Sound: Falcon *banks and applies all thrust in a desperate run to escape the doomed battle station.*

LANDO: When that reactor overloads, this whole place is finished. Pour it on, pour it on!

SCENE 6-14A   INTERIOR DEATH STAR

Sound: Background tumult as Imperials seek to escape the doomed station.

LUKE: Father . . . *(INDICATES EFFORT OF DRAGGING HIMSELF OVER TO VADER'S BODY)* Can you hear me?

VADER: Luke, help me take off this mask.

LUKE: But you'll die.

VADER: Just for once, let me look upon you with my own eyes.

SCENE 6-14B   INTERIOR DEATH STAR

Sound: Latches and seals being opened, as Luke removes the various modules of Vader's helmet, under next.

LUKE: *(INDICATING HE'S FINISHED)* There, Father.

ANAKIN: Ahh. That's good. Now . . . go, my son. Leave me, while there's still time to save yourself.

LUKE: No. We're taking the Emperor's shuttle together. I have to save you.

ANAKIN: You have saved me, Luke. Tell your sister . . . you were right about me.

LUKE: Father . . . I won't leave you.

ANAKIN: I'm proud that you've grown into the man . . . I once wanted to be . . .

LUKE: Father? . . . Father! . . .

SCENE 6-15 ENDOR FOREST

Sound: Louder rumblings and closer explosions, the Death Star's swan song. Death Star fades. Endor forest comes up.

THREEPIO: Look, another explosion! Surely the Death Star can't endure many more.

LEIA: No. Nothing could.

HAN: Here comes the big one—there! This is the payoff!

Sound: A pounding in the sky like thunder, as the battle station vanishes in a final fireball.

THREEPIO: They did it!

EWOKS AND REBELS: CHEER AND EXULT IN VICTORY.

THREEPIO: The Death Star is utterly destroyed!

LEIA: Yes, it is.

HAN: Leia, I'm sure Luke wasn't on that thing when it blew.

LEIA: He wasn't.

HAN: Hmmm. You know?

LEIA: I can feel it.

HAN: You love him, don't you?

LEIA: Well . . . yes.

HAN: Fine. I understand. When he comes back I won't get in your way.

LEIA: Han, he's my brother.

HAN: Brother? Then you weren't . . . ? Then Luke isn't . . . ?

LEIA: Why don't you stop worrying about Luke and talk about yourself?

HAN: Me? Ummmm . . .

LEIA: And the way you feel about me. About how there aren't enough scoundrels in my life.

HAN: Look, Leia. When this war's over you go back to being an Alliance leader and I go back to being a guy with a starship for hire. A princess and a smuggler; the odds against the two of us— ["—making a go of it with that kind of difference between us are so high even I wouldn't take a chance on 'em."]

LEIA: Han? Han, "never tell me the odds." Just kiss me.

SCENE 6-16 ENDOR EXTERIOR, DUSK

Sound: Scene fades. Dusk in Ewokville comes up, with Endor sounds.

THREEPIO: *(MOVING ON)* Pardon me, Master Luke? The Ewoks' victory celebration will be starting momentarily.

LUKE: I'll be right along, Threepio.

THREEPIO: But first you're going to light Lord Vader's—that is, your father's—funeral pyre, sir?

LUKE: What could be more fitting? It's a night of lights. Ewok victory fires. Rebel fireworks. Even the last pieces of the Death Star burning up in the atmosphere.

THREEPIO: Put that way, Master Luke, it does sound appropriate.

Sound: The fluttering of the big torch, as Luke takes it and swings it to ignite the stacked pyre under Vader/Anakin's armor, under next.

LUKE: I burn his armor and with it the name of Darth Vader. May the name of Anakin Skywalker be a light that guides the Jedi for generations to come.

Sound: Luke is setting the wood afire. It crackles and flares, under next.

THREEPIO: Master Luke, General Calrissian and the others are due at any moment.

LUKE: I'll be right along. *(TO HIS FATHER)* Rest well, Father. The Force is with you.

SCENE 6-17   TREETOP VILLAGE, EXTERIOR

Sound: Brief transition to the Ewok village, victory celebration in full swing.

LANDO: *(MOVING ON)* Han! Chewie! There you are!

CHEWBACCA: SNARLS A WOOKIEE GREETING.

HAN: Hey, Lando! You did it, right? You kept your word?

LANDO: What?

HAN: "Not a scratch," you said. You'd bring back the *Falcon* without a scratch on her.

THREEPIO: *(OFF)* They're over here, Master Luke.

LANDO: Well . . . nothing that's left on her is scratched. All the scratched parts got knocked off along the way.

HAN: "Knocked off?"

LEIA: Han, buck up. Here come Luke and Threepio.

THREEPIO: *(MOVING ON)* And look! Artoo-Detoo, and fully functional again.

ARTOO: DOES A VIVACIOUS GREETING TRILL.

THREEPIO: Artoo, when I tell the Ewoks the story of today's events I shall give you full credit for helping me accomplish my mission.

ARTOO: PUGNACIOUS OBJECTION TO THREEPIO'S SLANT ON THINGS.

THREEPIO: What d'you mean, you were the one who saved the day? All you managed to do was get your circuits fried when you— ["—so carelessly permitted yourself to be shot."]

LUKE: Threepio, I'm sure there'll be enough acclaim for everyone.

THREEPIO: I heartily agree with you sir.

ARTOO: BLAAATS HIS TRUCULENCE.

LANDO: Luke, sorry to hear about . . . your father.

LUKE: Thanks, Lando.

LANDO: But take a deep breath, Luke. That's freedom in the air.

Sound: The Ewok festivities, in the background, pick up tempo.

LANDO: Come on. *(MOVING OFF)* The party's starting.

HAN: That's for me. Chewie, grab us a good spot.

CHEWBACCA: GROWLS THAT HE WILL, MOVING OFF.

HAN: Ready, Luke?

LUKE: Be right along, Han.

LEIA: Don't be long . . . brother. Han has to explain how he wants to make you an uncle.

HAN: What? Hey, now wait a second.

LEIA: Let's go, Han.

HAN: *(BEING LED OFF BY LEIA)* "Uncle?" I never said . . . you never told me we . . . nobody mentioned anything about . . .

LEIA: *(MOVING OFF)* Stop worrying. We'll make it up as we go along.

THREEPIO: Pardon me, Master Luke, may I ask why you are staring into the darkness? What are you looking at?

LUKE: Not "what;" "who." Three comrades-in-arms. Obi-Wan Kenobi, Master Yoda . . . and Anakin Skywalker.

THREEPIO: My photoreceptors must be malfunctoning, sir. I don't see anything.

LUKE: But they're here. And they'll never be far from us. Their fire is back in the universe. Let it burn high and bright, to be seen by friend and foe. The Jedi have returned.

Music: Closing theme up under credits.

NARRATOR: CLOSING CREDITS.

ABOUT THE AUTHOR

BRIAN DALEY is the author of numerous works of science fiction and fantasy, including the Coramonde and Alacrity Fitzhugh books. He also scripted the National Public Radio serial adaptations of *Star Wars* and *The Empire Strikes Back*, dramatic recordings for Disneyland/ Buena Vista, and a number of animated TV episodes.

In collaboration with his friend and fellow Del Rey novelist James Luceno—using the pen name Jack McKinney—Brian co-wrote the *Robotech*, *Sentinels*, and *Black Hole Travel Agency* series.

Brian was in recent years laboring over an SF saga that's grown in the telling. Until his untimely death in March 1996, he and his longtime companion, historical novelist Lucia St. Clair Robson, lived in a quiet riverside community near Annapolis, Maryland.

STAR WARS

THE ORIGINAL RADIO DRAMA

By Brian Daley

You've seen the movie. But you've only heard half the story!

• How did Princess Leia and the Rebels get the plans for the Death Star?

• Just what was so dangerous about Beggar's Canyon?

• What kept Han Solo from double-crossing Luke and Ben?

• What compelled Princess Leia to join the Rebellion?

Learn the answers to these questions and many others in this original script of the acclaimed US radio dramatisation. A behind-the-scenes introduction by the script's author Brian Daley takes you into the recording studio with Mark Hamill, Anthony Daniels and others. This original script, with dialogue never heard on air, is the missing chapter in the history of a tale that began a long time ago in a galaxy far, far away...

THE ORIGINAL RADIO DRAMA

By Brian Daley

Scenes the movie never showed you...

- The Imperials discover the planetary probe evidence that leads them to the Rebel base.

- Luke's last minute rendezvous with his X-wing squadron during the battle of Hoth — on foot...

- Inside Yoda's cave on Luke's first morning of training in the mysterious ways of the Jedi.

You've seen the movie. You've read the book. But the radio drama is the only place to find these and other exciting new scenes and extra information on the events of *The Empire Strikes Back*, the second instalment in the acclaimed *Star Wars* series. A behind-the-scenes introduction by the script's author Brian Daley takes you into the recording studio with Mark Hamill, Anthony Daniels, Billy Dee Williams, John Lithgow and others. Follow the Rebel Alliance once more in their epic struggle across a galaxy far, far away...

THE ART OF *STAR WARS* GALAXY VOLUME 2

Written & edited by Gary Gerani

All-new art! All-new visions! All-new excitement!

Journey back to a galaxy far, far away in this second all-star collection of new artwork based on the *Star Wars* trilogy – the most enduring and popular film saga of our time.

Over seventy of today's greatest comic and fantasy illustrators provide new visions of the *Star Wars* galaxy, offering their personal interpretation of the movies' imagery, and recollections of the impact the trilogy had on them and their work. In addition to volume one, this volume also features expanded coverage of the production, promotional and merchandising art that has been produced for the film and its countless spin-off products.

Featuring the work of fan-favourite artists Jack 'King' Kirby, Dave Gibbons, Kelley Jones, John Bolton and Jim Starlin (along with many others), this book is a must for all film buffs, art aficionados, comic fans and *Star Wars* enthusiasts alike.

Also available from **Titan Books**

THE ART OF STAR WARS
RETURN OF THE JEDI

A lavish, full-colour volume that commemorates the creative genius
and technical wizardry behind *Return of the Jedi*, the third film in the
Star Wars trilogy. The book includes the complete script of the film by
George Lucas and Lawrence Kasdan, illustrated with hundreds of
sketches, storyboards, matte paintings, blueprints, production
paintings and costume designs.

Highlights include:

- Model construction of the new Death Star.
- Exterior and interior development of Jabba's palace.
- Blueprints and sketches of the Imperial shuttle design.
- Jabba's sail barge, from early sketches to live-action stills.
- The Moon of Endor, from construction of the Ewok village to
creation of the Ewoks themselves.
- New Rebel and Imperial vehicles, including the speeder bikes and
Admiral Ackbar's ship.

Also in this series:
THE ART OF STAR WARS - A NEW HOPE
THE ART OF STAR WARS - THE EMPIRE STRIKES BACK